HOW TO LEARN – HOW TO TEACH

Easily, Naturally, Successfully

By

Overcoming the Seven Barriers to Comprehension

Parent's & Student's
Edition

Revised 2014

Roger E. Boswarva CPT & Virginia Koenig CPT

ABILITY PRESS
New York

ISBN 978-0-9820727-3-8
Library of Congress Control Number: 2015935327

Ability Press: www.abilitypress.com
www.howtolearn-howtoteach.com

ACKNOWLEDGMENTS

There are some special folks who deserve notice for contribution to this book.

Our wonderful editor, who has the sharpest editing eye we've ever worked with and who was gracious enough to let us have some things the way we wanted them to be even though she saw them differently☺

Jeanmarie Martin
A WAY WITH WORDS
Proofreading & Editorial Services
(615) 895-7332
www.AWAYWITHWORDS.name
readydex@aol.com

Our cover illustrator and design wizard. We knew what we wanted and he came up with the goods. And he was a pleasure to work with.

Tom Cardamone
TCA Graphics Inc
Phone 239.514.3661
Fax 239.566.2659
tomsart4526@aol.com

Our photographer for Virginia's back cover photo, who really knows his business,

Greg Kinch
Greg Kinch Photography Inc.
greg@kinch.com   www.kinch.com
New York: 212.988.5210   Miami: 305.433.7136
Fax: 866.654.8135

ABOUT THE AUTHORS

Two of the world's leading learning performance experts . . .

Roger E. Boswarva and Virginia Koenig have spent their lives educating and benefiting others. For Roger, it began as a young man more than five decades ago when, as a swim champ in Australia, he began coaching the lads in his local surf life saving club's competition team. Virginia began her coaching and educating career in corporate America.

Roger is the Chairman and Founding Partner of Ability Consultants, Inc. and Management Science Associates and a management scientist of forty years experience in corporate, executive, and champion athlete performance improvement. As a Fellow of the British Institute of Management, he conducted management training and led seminars and symposia on executive and corporate performance improvement for the BIM, and the Management Center Europe, Brussels. Now retired from academia and international consulting to major corporations, he has spent the last ten years codifying the results of fifty years of research into aspects of human performance including the ability to learn. He is a Certified Performance Technologist with the International Society for Performance Improvement.

Virginia is trained in the Montessori Method of education. An avid tutor, she has spent the last several years as a volunteer tutor with Literacy Partners, a not-for-profit organization serving adults who failed in the conventional educational system but who have realized a need to improve, become literate, and earn their GED. She has spent twenty-five years in corporate Human Resources, specializing in employee benefits and training. She holds the Certified Employee Benefits Specialist designation from the Wharton School of Business and the International Foundation of Employee Benefit Plans, and is a Certified Performance Technologist with the International Society for Performance Improvement. In 1997, she joined Mr. Boswarva in establishing Ability Consultants, Inc. to specialize in ability and performance improvement for executives and organizational teams, and is currently the company president. She is the Founding President of the New York Environs Chapter of the International Society for Performance Improvement.

Praise for . . . .

How to Learn – How to Teach
Overcoming the Seven Barriers to Comprehension

Your book *How to Teach – How to Learn* is **simply exceptional**.
I have read it once through and found it extremely inspiring, especially the section on appreciation. The book's superb concept, flowing literacy and illuminating examples have significant positive impact. It is definitely an eye-opener for anyone fortunate enough to study it. I will definitely read it several times more as you recommend.
Our educators and trainers desperately need this material to enlighten dull classrooms and make teaching fun and rewarding again. Our children, their parents, students, graduates, employees and employers all need the vital data in your book to realize and fully reach their true potential.

> Malcolm Bugler
> *YMCA Board Member, South East Branch, Rochester NY*

I think the book is **great for home schooling parents**, but I see it as **a great resource for professional development for teachers**. It is great. The concepts and exercises are wonderful, thought-provoking and truly relevant.

> Kevin Hanks
> *Principals Recruitment and Development, Edison Schools, Inc.*
> *A former Teacher, School Principal, Assistant Superintendent, and Director of Human Resources for Southern Westchester Board of Cooperative Education Services*

WOW! What a wonderful manual! I'm what you describe in the book as the dyslexic type. The book was quite validating for me. I do simply have a different way of learning. I'm sure I'll get tremendous amounts out of this manual. **The material is all there.** Thank you for taking the time to do it right . . . and the wonderful stories.

> Karla, *home schooling country mom*

How to Learn – How to Teach **is an eye-opener**. I had a big AHA! moment looking at the definition of *success*, and a physical reaction. It's amazing how many words I have skimmed by thinking—yeah, yeah, yeah, I can figure that out. Not a good strategy, I now see.

> Marlaina Gayle
> *Columnist, The Province Newspaper & Contributor to CBC Newsworld/BCTV News Hour, Vancouver Former Press Secretary and Media Liaison for the Loyal Opposition, Government of British Columbia, Canada.*

The materials in this book are an amazing revelation.
When I did my first exercise from *How to Learn – How to Teach*, I experienced the astounding effect of the Barriers to Comprehension. It created a profound awareness in me of just how damaging these barriers can be. *How to Learn – How to Teach* definitely contains the answers on how to learn, and also the key to personal productivity and success in life.

> Christopher Calta
> *Manager College of Customer Service, JetBlue Airways University*

Our Purpose

This book was written because we wish that all who want to learn, be literate and competent may fully accomplish it.

To this end we have dedicated ourselves to helping all who share this dream to fulfill it; whether they be students, parents, teachers, executives, coaches, humanitarians or philanthropists.

Virginia and I are available for one-on-one counsel and guidance, and help in the form of lectures or other training and address to groups.

For schools, home education groups, colleges, universities, non-profits, corporations or professional organizations, special editions of this book and discount rates for bulk orders are available.

Please contact us at:
www.abilityconsultants.com, or rboswarva@abilityconsultants.com or
vkoenig@abilityconsultants.com or
WWW.HOWTOLEARN-HOWTOTEACH.COM

Mailing address:
162 West 13th Street
Suite 1
New York NY 10011
Telephone: 212 924 2619

TABLE OF CONTENTS

Part One

Part Two

The Workbook of Exercises . . . 67

These are the exercises we have created that address your basic abilities related to study and learning ≈ Recovering the ability to knowingly do what you are doing when you are doing it, and to do it under your aware control ≈ The action of knowingly exercising: the key to empowering ability (it's what athletes do when they train).

The Workbook has been created as a stand-alone volume. Its contents are:

Endnotes . . . 98

Additional Information to Explain, Clarify or Verify Material in this Manual

The Index . . .

The list of Who's and What's and their location in this manual

INTRODUCTION

WHY THIS BOOK WAS WRITTEN

WHAT'S IN IT FOR YOU

We all want to do the best we can, achieve the most we can, help our families, friends and loved ones the most we can. In short, we want to succeed at the highest level in all our endeavors, and we also want this for our children.

To achieve this, we need to harness the most basic of our abilities: the ability to learn.

As parents, if we want our children to do well in school and in life, this material is essential.

Research shows that those individuals who learn easily also succeed easily. Indeed, the ability to learn is an essential ingredient of success.

It is to be noted that learning is more than what you see attempted in our schools and universities. It is a life-long process that is part of every activity or endeavor we engage in.

Your level of success in life very much depends on your ability to interface with life's activities and opportunities, to perceive them correctly, to understand them and then respond in an optimum manner. And that very much involves the exercise of the learning faculty we all innately have.

In essence, all of life is a learning curve.

However, many, many folk have real difficulty learning and don't realize the extent of their difficulty. The vast majority of folk are not learning at anything like their true capacity. Virtually everyone has some degree of learning barrier impeding their ability to easily learn at their optimum level. And this, of course, is reducing their achievement in life's endeavors.

Research has revealed the Seven Barriers to Comprehension that impede or block the ability to learn.

Tragically, these Seven Barriers to Comprehension are in place and teachers and parents unknowingly commit them on virtually every child or student in our schools and universities in today's system. And the result is the poor literacy levels and failing grades we read so much about in the press. Homeschooling parents who are unaware of this material will also tragically commit this error on their children.

None of us want this—for ourselves, or our children.

This book has the answers to this tragic situation. Used properly, the materials in this book are the key to your success and the success of your children.

If you want to win in life and at all of life's endeavors, this book is for you.

This is why this book has been written.

Roger E. Boswarva
rboswarva@abilityconsultants.com
&
Virginia Koenig
vkoenig@abilityconsultants.com

New York
December 29, 2006

ABOUT THIS BOOK

This book has been written for the average mom and dad, student and teacher.

It is not written as an academic tome. It does not attempt to be one.

We have presented here what we find our clients and other users of this material see as being easily observable, self evident truths. It is all logical, simple stuff when you look at it. Stuff about which we constantly hear folks saying, "Of course, it is all so logical when you see it pointed out!"

It is the result of empirical research, test, and observation: not theoretical musings.

We invite you to inspect, evaluate and test these observations and findings for yourself.

We do not resort to other "authority" or citation of others' works to bolster the credence of what we present here. That would make it too cumbersome for easy use.

We invite you to observe the obvious and to test it for yourself.

THE IMPORTANCE OF THIS BOOK

It is Attainable That We Learn With Full Comprehension One Hundred Percent of What is Presented to Us and That We Have the Ability to Masterfully Apply All That is Learned During Our Studies

This is the reason for this book being written. Properly used, the materials and principles in it will accomplish what is stated above.

This is a vitally important, much needed book, as demonstrated by The National Assessment of Adult Literacy conducted by the U.S. Department of Education.

An article in *The New York Times* dated December 16, 2005, reported as follows:

> The average American college graduate's literacy in English declined significantly over the past decade, according to results of a nationwide test released yesterday.
>
> The National Assessment of Adult Literacy, given in 2003 by the Department of Education is the nation's most important test of how well Americans can read.
>
> When the test was last administered, in 1992, 40 percent of the nation's college graduates scored at the proficient level, meaning that they were able to read lengthy, complex English texts and draw complicated inferences. But on the 2003 test, only 31 percent of the graduates demonstrated those high-level skills. There were 26.4 million college graduates.
>
> Of the college graduates tested in 2003, 69 percent failed to demonstrate proficiency, with 53 percent of the total tested scoring at the intermediate level and 14 percent scoring at the basic level, meaning they could only read and understand short, commonplace prose texts.
>
> Three percent of college graduates who took the test in 2003, representing some 800,000 Americans, demonstrated "below basic" literacy, meaning

they could not perform more than the simplest skills, like locating easily identifiable information in short prose.

These are rather shocking facts when you consider that this is the literacy level of *college graduates*. Of those not getting to college, the statistics are horrific. One hears of ninety-percent illiteracy rates in some inner-city areas.

Quite obviously, something is amiss in or with the system we are now using to educate our children.

This book will plug that hole if properly applied.

On this point, let me tell you a true, sad story from my own personal history.

I was born in 1936, my sister, Marie, in 1938. The result was that the critical early years of our schooling were during World War II and the time of shortages following the war. Our hometown, Sydney, Australia, was very much on a war-footing as it had been attacked by submarine, and the suburb where we lived shelled from sea by those subs.

At about age seven or eight, my sister found herself is a class that was grossly overcrowded — simply not enough space in the classroom. The solution of the teachers was to take the three brightest children in the class and "promote" them forward into the next higher school grade group, which classroom had some desk space. The result was that my sister missed a whole year of curriculum at a critical early school learning age. She was being presented with material that was a year of schooling more advanced than where she actually was in terms of progress in her education.

The outcome of this was that Marie crashed from being a star, bright, head-of-the-class student to being the dunce of the class. Real rot set in. She, and my parents, actually came to the conclusion she was dull. And as Marie grew older, finding she couldn't read, write or do math adequately, not only did she consider herself "dull," but relatively worthless.

Tragic self-image, self-worth, negative conclusions developed.

When I look back at this now, I am much saddened and a little outraged, for what I see is that a bright young star, a gorgeous person, had her dreams, aspirations and life ruined by some educators who didn't understand their business correctly. (The specific error and barrier to comprehension the teachers foisted on this young girl is shown in Chapter Six.)

Fifteen years ago, I was back in Australia on a consulting assignment and visited my sister with the material that is now written in this book. With it, I was able to recover her missed education, restore for her the truth of her ability to learn and, along with it, the truth of her self-worth and value as a wonderful Being.

Today, as a very active senior citizen, she is an avid learner, active in all kinds of new things in her community, and even writes articles for the local newspaper. This from a person who for most of her adult life considered herself to be dull and semi-literate.

You will read some other examples of faulty "teaching" practices in this manual that we should seek to eliminate from our educational system. But most important, this manual reveals those imperative positives that must be known and applied as part of the practice of educating our children.

A vital one follows.

It is extremely important that you properly recognize, acknowledge, validate, honor and appreciate any wins, insights or sudden AHA's! We call these cognitions. It is a word that is not in all dictionaries, but it means "to become suddenly or extremely aware or cognizant of something". A big breakthrough in knowledge and/or ability to perform would be such an event; and all such wins must be honored and appreciated so they can be fully empowered and continue to be under your or the student's knowing future control. There is an old saying: *"Use it or lose it."*

Appendix 6 gives you further explanation of the reason it is important to write up such wins and have them properly honored and appreciated.

Appendices 5 and 7 contain very important and useful procedures for fully validating, stabilizing and empowering big wins and ascensions of awareness or ability.

The knowledge presented in this manual has been hard won. The fruits of fifty years of direct personal research, apart from the distillation of the wisdom of the ancients and many others who have addressed these subjects of study and learning, are contained here.

Of particular value has been the work of Alan C. Walter.

I am fortunate to have known Alan Walter since 1962. We were both champion athletes at the time, he a professional Australian Rules football player and I a swimmer. We were each independently involved in research into improving athletic performance. Over the years, we found that the factors that determine superior athletic performance also affected all other activities of life, and we began to apply these discoveries to all other areas of activity and in particular to the enhancement of human potential overall.

In 1994, after we had both traveled the world independently pursuing our careers and research, I became aware of the particular breakthroughs Alan had made in the field of human potential and performance at the Advanced Coaching and Leadership Center, St. Jo, Texas, and I embraced his particular discoveries in those areas. (See http://www.knowledgism.com)

Therefore, in addition to my own work, and that of my co-author Virginia, we have included applicable materials from the works of Alan Walter that will vastly assist you who seek greater knowledge, improved ability to perform, and who also wish to succeed in attaining your life dreams and aspirations.

Roger E. Boswarva

HOW TO USE THIS MANUAL

This manual has been set up to be used in either of two ways:

1. As a book that any parent or educator can read in order to obtain the vital knowledge needed to successfully facilitate the learning and education of their children.
2. As a study course to show all students how to truly learn when studying, along with how to avoid the Barriers to Comprehension and learning that plague so many.

It contains vital knowledge for *all* individuals who want to be successful in their lives, careers, relationships and interests they wish to pursue.

For parents and educators, we recommend reading the manual once through to grasp the principles being presented; and then to go through the manual a second time, this time doing it as a study course using the Course Progress Checklist (next following this section) and the full set of Drills in the *Workbook of Exercises* located in the Appendix. In this way, a full comprehension of the material and the ability to optimally apply it will be obtained.

There is a datum in the realm of study, which is: The number of times over the material equals degree of certainty. So be prepared to restudy this manual a number of times.

Younger students or children beginning their studies would learn this material from their parents or educators as it is being applied to them. The principles would be passed on verbally as the need arises, thus making the student able to apply the knowledge in this book to learn successfully while engaging in study.

For mature or more experienced students, the best option would be to treat this manual as a study course and, at the first reading, use and follow the Course Progress Checklist (next following this section) and the full set of Drills in the *Workbook of Exercises* located in the Appendix. Ideally, this should be done with a study partner and/or study coach for the optimum results, though the drills and exercises can be done "solo" by asking the questions or giving the commands to oneself directly off the page as you are reading it.

HOW TO LEARN – HOW TO TEACH

Easily, Naturally and Successfully
by
Overcoming the Seven Barriers to Comprehension

Course Progress Checklist

The How to Learn – How to Teach Course has been designed to deliver the ability to both learn to and teach at a level of mastery. As such, you will be introduced to some remarkable concepts, techniques, exercises and processes.

There is a sequence to learning new material and taking it all the way to mastery.

The sequence goes somewhat like this: contact, orientation, familiarity, learning the nomenclature of key items; then attempts at applications, practice, re-reading, re-studying, re-orientation, significances, some application experiences, lots of mistakes, failures, occasional wins, re-study, de-bugging, gaining full comprehension of nomenclature and key items, sub-items, words and terms of the subject, more practice, wins, practice again, bigger wins, complete re-study, more practice, application, consistent wins in application, mastery.

How long does it take to master a subject? As long as it takes. It takes forever if you put off doing it.

Some people are experienced in taking areas of their life to mastery; some have never taken anything or any area of their life to mastery. Those who have never taken anything or any area of their life to mastery are those who have knowingly or unknowingly chosen to be mediocre.

As one gains familiarity with all parts of the subject, one also gains awareness, knowledge and experience. The higher your awareness, the more the new knowledge and increased experience will collide with previous decisions and ways you have made yourself unaware, and old false knowledge, false ideas, false destructive precepts and similar failed earlier experiences will come to view.

The secret to mastering anything is to maintain contact and connection with it and to keep yourself focused on an area until you have mastered it. And you must be willing to use gradients of learning. So many people quit when they hit their first failure. Failure is always part of the learning process; failure lets you know there is something you do not know or understand.

HOW TO SUCCEED ON THIS COURSE AND IN LIFE

1. Invest or allocate enough time to fully master each piece until you have mastered the whole – this can be easily observed by consistently demonstrating competence in what you are studying.

2. Invest or allocate enough focused effort.

3. Invest or allocate enough focused attention*.

4. Create enough focused space and time to produce the product you desire.

5. Break up each area into specifics, and master each specific.

6. Be true to yourself and your dreams.

7. Keep persisting until you have hit your TARGET and have attained fully what you promised yourself and others.

ORDER OF MATERIAL TO BE STUDIED

This Course Progress Checklist is laid out in the most optimum sequence of study actions for you to learn the skills and acquire the knowledge you want. This is important, because there is an optimum gradient and correct sequence of learning and skills acquisition through which a student goes in order to learn any subject most easily.

Note that you should be ready to use *Celebration of Regained Abilities, States and Wins Procedure*; and the *Future Alignment Process*, as appropriate **at any time** you or your study partner have a major win, regained ability or recovered state of being. It is important to recognize, validate, own and honor such wins. These procedures are located in the Appendix.

SECTION 1 PRELIMINARIES

_____ Write out your intention and optimum scenario for doing this course. *Note*: be prepared to amend and/or upgrade your intention and optimum scenario as you progress through this course.

YOUR COURSE PROGRESS CHECKLIST

_____ 1. Read: "How to Use This Manual" at the front of the book.

_____ 2. Read: Chapter One — The ability to learn is a natural ability we all have.

_____ 3. Do: Rehabilitation of Certainty on the Ability to Learn Procedure (at end of Chapter 1)

_____ 4. Read: Chapter 2 — The Barriers to Comprehension

_____ 5. Read: Chapter 3 — Learning Barrier One

_____ 6. a. Do: Drill One (Part 1) *All drills are in the Workbook Section of the Appendix.*

_____ b. Do: Drill One (Part 2)

_____ c. Do: Drill One (Part 3)

_____ 7. Read: Chapter 4 — Learning Barrier Two

_____ 8. a. Do: Drill Two (Part 1)

_____ b. Do: Drill Two (Part 2) Using the **Clean Slate Handling Learning Drill,** Clean Slate the words: *study, learning,* and the concept/action of *studying to learn"*
(The Clean Slate process should be used as needed at any time during your course, and on *all* key words, phrases and concepts)

_____ 9. Read: Chapter 5, page 20 only.

_____ 10. Do: Drill Three on page 21.

_____ 11. Read: Complete Chapter 5 — Learning Barrier Three

_____ 12. Do: Drill Four on page 29.

_____ 13. Read: Chapter 6 — Learning Barrier Four

_____ 14. Do: Drill Five on page 35 (Part 1) and page 36 (Part 2).

_____ 15. Read: Chapter 7 — Learning Barrier Five

_____ 16. Do: Drill Six on page 41 (Part 1) and page 42 (Part 2).

_____ 17. Read: Chapter 8 — Learning Barrier Six

_____ 18. Do: Drill Seven

_____ 19. Read: Chapter 9 — Learning Barrier Seven

_____ 20. a. Do: Drill Eight (Part 1)

_____ b. Do: Drill Eight (Part 2)

_____ c. Do: Drill Eight (Part 3)

_____ 21. Read: Chapter 10 — Mastering the Learning Process — How Learning Masters Operate

CONGRATULATIONS — you have completed the How to Learn – How to Teach Course. Now strive for excellence and mastery of the application of what you have learned and accomplished here.

30 December, 2005   Roger E. Boswarva

CHAPTER ONE

LEARNING AND STUDY ARE DIFFERENT

"All men by nature desire knowledge"
Aristotle (384–322 B.C.)

The ability to learn is a faculty we all have. Young children do it naturally.

The big question is: What gets in its way? Why do folks so often have difficulty in learning?

As a parent, teacher or student, knowing the answer to these questions should be of keen interest to you; and you will be happy to know this book contains those answers.

Similarly, there are factors that impede a student's ability to engage in the action of studying; and the answers to remedying these impediments are available in the *Professional Edition* of this book.

The Action of Studying versus The Ability to Learn

Please observe what has been written above. We are addressing *two* subjects:

    a) the action of studying *and*
    b) the ability to learn.

Each has a different set of distinctive barriers that prevent a student from properly and successfully doing these actions.

In truth, while many see these actions of studying and learning as being "the same thing," they are in actuality quite different. They are related, but different.

Study is an action one engages in, in order to learn, though one can learn, as young children do, by simple perception or action without studying.

For our purposes here, *study* is simply defined as:

1. The act or process of applying the mind in order to acquire knowledge, as by reading, investigating, experimenting, etc.

2. Attentive scrutiny.

Though this is something you should more fully address by reading the full definition in a proper big dictionary (pocket dictionaries often skip too much).

The word *learn* is defined as: To gain knowledge, comprehension, or mastery of through experience or study. (Again you should consult a dictionary for all of the senses of its definition.)

We have addressed both of these subjects, learning *and* studying, and show you how to remove the impediments or blocks to them, as well as what positive steps you can take that will increase the speed, ease and power of learning for your children, students and even yourself. However, for the Home-Schooling parent and students we have limited the *Parent's & Student's Edition* to the learning barriers. The barriers to being able to study are addressed in the *Professional Edition* of this book.

As parents and educators we have a duty to our children, and that is, as teachers and leaders, we must conduct our educating of them in a manner which harnesses and facilitates their natural ability to learn and does not impede them.

This book is the definitive manual of how to do that successfully.

It defines the Seven Barriers to Comprehension that block learning and gives you the positive answers for overcoming them wherever they have occurred. It also gives you the answers needed to prevent them from happening in the first place, or from happening again in the future.

Additionally, our expanded professional edition delineates the Twelve Vital Fundamentals which, if violated, result in a student being unable to fully and successfully engage in studying, and it gives positive remedies for their repair and maintenance where necessary.

Personal Methods of Learning

This book also reveals a very important point that must be made here relative to studying and learning, and it is this: While it is true we are each gifted with the ability to learn, *the more important point is that* **we each have our own personal method of learning.**

Unfortunately, this is something that gets trampled on in the conventional educational system of our schools. Students are too often made to sit still, be quiet and simply record. Their natural instinct to carry out their own learning method is crushed.

This is something my good friend, Alan C. Walter, observed among mature students and adults at the Advanced Coaching & Leadership Center, St. Jo, Texas, a few years ago. (Other educators have also made this observation and commented on it.)

The students in question didn't like studying, and said they had great difficulty studying and learning. Many had come to the conclusion that they were "poor students" or "couldn't learn." Yet these individuals had all successfully held down jobs and performed in accordance with the norms of society.

Investigating this, Walter found that these individuals had all had successes in learning, but that their individual, personal styles of learning had been interfered with or suppressed in school, with the result that they had given up trying to learn in that environment. Studying and learning had become a failing, painful endeavor for them.

There is a remedy for this, which we will give you shortly, but there are some points on the issue of learning styles to be made first.

Styles of Learning

In simple terms, it has been found that some students prefer to learn "aurally"; they like to *hear* what they have to learn. Others are "visual" and like to be able to *read* or *see* what they have to learn, while others are *tactile doers* who feel the need to experience and discover by *doing*. Some students achieve this by repeating what they have to learn or by writing it down as a form of *doing* it. (Sometimes the doing is satisfied by underlining or highlighting key things to be learned while reading.)

Discovery Learning & Inquiry-Based Learning

In essence these are different names for the experiential *doing* style of learning. Prof. Robert Lee Moore introduced this style of education into the Science and Mathematics classes at the University of Texas beginning in 1920. It became known as the "Moore Method" and was based on the use of a list of axioms or already known facts, questions to resolve and results to obtain. Employing this sequence caused the student to uncover or discover the essentials of the knowledge needed to comprehend the subject or area being addressed.

This system of course requires that correct earlier gradients of knowledge be in possession of the student. (See Chapter 6: *By-passed Gradients*.)

The essence of this educational practice was that it engaged the students in *doing*. It also put the student at *cause* as a source of developing their own knowledge rather than holding them at effect of indoctrination.

So successful was this method of education that other educators further developed the process, putting their own twists on it, giving it different names.

Maria Montessori and Rudolph Steiner also developed this style of education in Europe in the period before and after World War One. (See later in this chapter.)

Three-Dimensional Learners

Many students are "three-dimensional" learners, which we discuss in-depth later in this chapter. (A good Internet site devoted to this is: www.3dlearner.com)

Some students like to get the theory and complete instructions on a subject before they attempt to do anything. Others prefer to learn, as above, by doing: they want the minimum of theory and instruction sufficient for them to be able to get into action and learn by *doing*. These latter type students are the great experimenters who learn by action or doing and figuring it out for themselves.

Michael Faraday, the great nineteenth-century British scientist, is a case in point. With no formal scientific education, he abandoned his apprenticeship as a bookbinder to follow his inquisitive instincts to become a laboratory assistant at the Royal Society working for the chemist Sir Humphry Davy. Faraday learned by doing and by experimentation. It is he who today is credited as being the father of modern electricity. It is he who first liquefied gases, invented the electric motor and discovered electromagnetic induction and a host of other scientific discoveries.

Thomas Edison only had three months formal schooling. He was dismissed from school by his teacher for being "overactive." Taught to read by his mother, Edison thereafter educated himself by visiting the local library. But his obvious learning method was that of experimentation and doing, as is demonstrated by his career as an inventor.

You might be surprised to learn how many immensely successful, top businessmen were poor students or flunked out of school. A May 13, 2003, article in *Fortune Magazine* cited the following innovators and leaders as all being dyslexic. Sir Richard Branson (Virgin Records, Virgin Airlines), Charles Schwab, John Chambers (Cisco), Craig McCaw (pioneer of the cell phone industry), Paul Orfalea (Founder of Kinko's) is a partial list of over a dozen cited. Needless to say their learning style was seriously impeded by the current educational system.

The hallmark of these individuals is that they are all creative, all innovators and all "think outside of the box" of the norm. Being regimented and made to sit still, be quiet and simply absorb by rote what the conventional schooling methods attempted to implant in them suppressed their natural learning method. These types of students either rebel or become despondent in such a system. Their free will and sovereignty is impeded and crushed.

Conventional wisdom has held dyslexia to be a "disability." In actuality it is not correctly understood.

Dyslexia May Well be the Mark of A Higher Level
Of
Natural Ability

Far from being a disability, dyslexia may well be the mark of a higher level of natural ability not expressed by the "normal" student who is content, or forced, to learn only by rote.

The *Fortune Magazine* article cites the use of this higher ability by the individuals covered:

> Bill Dreyer, an inventor and biologist at Caltech, recalls a dinner party conversation years ago in which he told a colleague how his dyslexic brain works: "I think in 3-D Technicolor pictures instead of words." "You what?" replied the incredulous colleague. The two argued the rest of the night how that was possible.

> Dreyer believes that thinking in 3-D pictures enabled him to develop groundbreaking theories about how antibodies are made, and then to invent one of the first protein-sequencing machines, which helped launch the human genome revolution. "I was able to see the machine in my head and rotate valves and actually see the instrumentation," he says. "I don't think of dyslexia as a deficiency. It's like having CAD (computer-aided design) in your brain. I bet these other guys see business in 3-D too."

> In his office, John Chambers (Cisco) goes from wounded to animated as he heads to the dry-erase board to show that's exactly what he does. "I can't explain why, but I just approach problems differently," he says. "It's very easy for me to jump from A to Z. I picture a chess game on a multiple-layer dimensional cycle and almost play it out in my mind. But it's not a chess game. It's business. I don't make moves one at a time. I can usually anticipate the potential outcome and where the Y's in the road will occur."

The famed scientist-inventor, Nikola Tesla, also had this ability to visualize his inventions holographically as 3-D working models that he could actually operate and, as needed, deconstruct, amend and reconstruct. (Wickipedia.com has a wonderful write-up on Tesla's spectacular accomplishments for those not familiar with the name at: http://en.wikipedia.org/wiki/Nikola_Tesla.)

It is this three-dimensional holographic perception that dyslexics often operate with that can give them difficulty reading two-dimensional imagery on paper.

Living & Learning Holographically

Some students not only operate holographically, as in the examples above, but *learn* holographically. We commonly find this with elite, champion athletes. They are quite holographic operating in life and in their method of learning. "Book learning" can be a little tiresome and difficult for these types of students. They like to be active and to "get into things." Learning is a fully experiential process for them, not just a theoretical ivory tower-type affair.

A description of holographic learning, living or operating might be a little difficult to convey to those who are not so inclined; rather like describing the smell of a rose to a person who has never had any sense of smell, or the beauty of a sunset to a person who has been sightless all his or her life. Remember the earlier example of Bill Dreyer describing to an incredulous colleague that his thinking is in "Three-Dimensional Technicolor instead of words."

For those who are holographic in their living and learning, the "pictures" in their minds are not flat nor particularly separate and apart from them; the images they perceive are fully three-dimensionally holographic, and the person can often be surrounded by the image if they choose. It is as though the image is at one with them, throughout them, or that they are present throughout the image.

Similarly, in life, their perception of the environment is often holographic in that they don't just see straight ahead where their eyes are looking; they often experience "being at, and with, what they are perceiving in the physical environment."

I remember hearing a star baseball slugger describing how, when he is "on," or "in the Zone," it's as though he is "with the ball as it is coming in from the pitcher." You'll often hear champion sports stars describe these magic moments when they were aware of everything "all around them," and they "had all the time in the world to act"; "opponents appear to be in slow motion." Folks often experience these kinds of perception changes on vacation when spanning marvelous, vast spaces or expanded vistas such as mountain ranges.

On inspection, we find this to be very much a natural spiritual perception phenomenon. It is not limited in the same manner as physical eyesight.

Investigation has found this ability to perceive or visualize in three-dimensional holographic terms to be more of a spiritual ability than a "mental" ability. The difficulty with this in our western society is that our culture is not very comfortable recognizing the true nature of our spiritual powers, and the terms of reference used are muddied and not clearly defined.

As Pierre Teilhard de Chardin wrote, "We are not human beings having a spiritual experience. We are spiritual beings having a human experience."

As parents and educators, we must be alert to the full, true spiritual nature as well as the learning styles of our students, and facilitate them both. Failure to do so will cause immense difficulty and damage to the student.

I am fortunate to have traveled the world and lived in a number of different cultures. This has exposed me to various and different understandings of what life is, who or what we are as living beings, and to the belief systems and practices that go along with those different views of life.

Western society's prevailing "scientific" view, along with some of its modern religious views, are often quite different than what is found in a study of these other cultures and also in our own history.

Going earlier, one finds the great sages and teachers of antiquity: Siddhartha Gautama (known now as The Buddha), Confucius, Socrates, Plato and Aristotle were all aware of their true spiritual nature and powers, and the truth that we are reincarnated beings who have lived before. This truth is, of course, well known as an experiential certainty in the Hindu and other Eastern religious cultures, and among the native societies of the world.

It is only in relatively recent times, a mere one hundred and fifty years or so, that the "scientific" notion was invented that we are not spiritual. The error of the scientific community, unfortunately, is that they only ever try to perceive, detect, measure or test spiritual phenomena by or with physical universe means and methods. We do not have reliable technology for that as yet. If you want to perceive, test and experience spiritual phenomena, the way to do it is to do what you do to perceive, test or experience anything else in your life: Do so directly with your natural faculties – and trust what you perceive.

As you do the drills and processes in this manual, you will have the opportunity to do this.

And these notions are not just the realm of the "New Age fraternity"; it is the stuff of mainstream science also. There is much work being done nowadays through research at leading universities into subjects such as consciousness, our true spiritual nature, and reincarnation.

A good example is the work of Dr. Jim B. Tucker, Medical Director of the Child and Family Psychiatric Clinic at the University of Virginia, and member of the University's Division of Perceptual Studies. His book, *Life Before Life: A Scientific Investigation of Children's Memories of Previous Lives,* has been hailed by his scientific peers.

In April 2006, a three-day symposium involving presentations of findings by forty distinguished investigators was held at the University of California, Berkeley, under the banner, "Spiritual Transformation: New Frontiers for Scientific Research."

Beyond Normal Perception

An article dated November 29, 2005, in the Science Times section of *The New York Times*, referred to this. The article reported on research carried out at the University of Virginia into the perception characteristics of the best baseball hitters.

The article opened with the comment, "Athletes on a hot streak often describe warps in space-time that Einstein did not anticipate: basketball hoops appearing as wide as hula hoops, tennis balls that seem to move in slow motion, golf outings in which the cups seem as easy to hit as manholes."

The article went on to say that the research found, "The changes in perception are apparently real . . . "

Based on my personal experience as an athlete and in dealing with other champion athletes, I can vouch for the existence of these perception capabilities "beyond the norm."

Another experience students quite often have is that of recovering the knowledge "they already knew." This is not uncommon, indeed, Plato wrote: "Searching and learning is a process of remembering." These phenomena were very well known to the ancients.

Socrates wrote, "A mind is a flame to be ignited, not a vessel to be filled."

This is something Dr. Maria Montessori, the founder of the Montessori educational method and international school system observed. As Dr. Montessori wrote in *Education for a New World*:

> Scientific observation has established that education is not what the teacher gives; education is a natural process spontaneously carried out by the human individual, and is acquired not by listening to words but by experiences upon the environment. The task of the teacher becomes that of preparing a series of motives of cultural activity, spread over a specially prepared environment, and then refraining from obtrusive interference. Human teachers can only help the great work that is being done, as servants help the master. Doing so, they will be witnesses to the unfolding of the human soul and to the rising of a New Man who will not be a victim of events, but will have the clarity of vision to direct and shape the future of human society.

The great Rudolph Steiner, the founder of the international Waldorf Schools system, made these same observations.

Socrates was not only famous for his "Socratic method" of education, which is the practice of asking questions of the student so as to educe answers and knowledge, but he is also famous for using different approaches for different individuals. Confucius also recognized that people learn in different ways with varying abilities.

Following at the end of this chapter is a remedial action that can be used for any student that considers he or she "is a bad student," "has trouble learning" or "cannot learn."

Cause and Effect in Learning

Parents and educators need to be alert to maintaining an optimum balance of the student being cause and effect when they are dealing with children and students engaged in the learning process. In a word, we should say, allowing the child to retain *sovereignty* or; put differently, we could express it is terms of whether the student is out-flowing, causative and creative—or is the student inflowing, constantly put at effect by being made to be a receipt-point of the teacher's out-flow and indoctrination.

It is an issue that has only recently been studied in conventional scientific circles, but what is being found is very valuable and somewhat amazing. Though it is true to say that practitioners in the fields of athletic performance and the human potential movement have led science on this issue by several decades.

Prevailing conventional wisdom on the issue of the development of our children is engaged in a dispute between two different doctrines: the question of whether it is "nurture" or "nature" that determines how a person develops. On inspection, and in practice, we find this to be a rather fallacious argument.

Both do have a degree of influence. But it is not an issue of either one or the other being the determining factor; they both *can* have an influence. *However, senior to both "nature" and "nurture" is the student's own volition, his or her own cause and ability to determine and direct his or her own affairs and destiny. This is the senior and determining factor in how a child develops.*

The Montessori Method is famous for getting this right.

Three Stages of Student Decline

Tragically, however, all too common is the circumstance wherein the child's volition, free will, sovereignty and right to choose for itself is suppressed and trampled on. The student or child is placed at effect in the learning environment and is overwhelmed and unable to causatively express itself.

This suppression of free will produces the following sequence of three effects, any one of which the student can get stuck in, and thus set the child's behavior and attitude:

a) first protest and/or rebellion, then,

b) propitiation and passivity which, if the overwhelming of the child's volition and sovereignty continues, results in

c) dejection, despondency and abandonment of any participation in the area connected to the abusive overwhelm.

Thus we can observe that when the environment (nature) and the nurturing influences are negatively overwhelming, they will have a determining affect on the child; but where the nature and nurture influences are positive, the child's own free will and choice are the determining factors in the child's development. Yes, the choices made by the child may be influenced, but the exercise of the child's own volition is the determining factor.

Dr. Bruce Lipton, Ph.D., the noted biologist and researcher at Stanford University and formerly at the University of Wisconsin Medical School, has done some stellar work which demonstrates that the DNA ("nature") really is not a determining factor in our development or behavior. It will determine some of our physical structure and form but that is all, and even some of that is determined by response to what is perceived by the free will of the individual. This is seen in athletes who shape and sculpt their bodies for their particular sport.

Lipton has written some wonderful papers for the layman that are available at his website: www.brucelipton.com. Of particular interest here is his paper under the tab "Conscious Parenting." The actual title and subject of the paper is "Nature, Nurture and Human Development."

What Lipton and others are showing is that each individual cell of the human body operates as though it is a whole sentient Being unto itself and, in alignment and concert with the other cells of the body, forms the composite of the body that functions in the manner we are familiar with. Research demonstrates that each cell perceives its environment and reacts to any toxicity, threat, nourishment or symbiotic relationship perceived beyond its outer membrane or skin. In other words, based on perception and analysis of what is perceived at or beyond the membrane, the cell will choose to retract away or even flee from or expand and move toward that which is perceived. The DNA content in the cell is shown not to be determining any action, but responds as a machine-like entity in accordance with the volition exhibited by the sentience *surrounding* the cell.

Thus we see volition is at play here: the decision to retract, flee or move toward. Based on these observations, Lipton has developed a highly workable and practical process that all can use, which is based on the positive determining of our environment and affairs.

Another related and very interesting change that was recently introduced, which altered the conventional wisdom of psychology and the social sciences, was revealed in an interview with Professor Martin E.P. Seligman, the (then) president of the American Psychological Association, in the April 28, 1998, edition of *The New York Times*, Science News section. The article begins:

> Psychologists rarely think much about what makes people happy. They focus on what makes them sad, on what makes them anxious. That is why psychology journals have published 45,000 articles in the last 30 years on depression, but only 400 on joy. . . . .

> It was not always like that. When psychology began developing as a profession, it had three goals: to identify genius, to heal the sick and to help people live better, happier lives. Over the last half century, however, it has focused almost entirely on pathology, taking the science of medicine, itself structured around disease, as its model. . . .

> 'That is an imbalance,' says Martin E.P. Seligman, the new president of the American Psychological Association, and one that he is determined to change. Dr. Seligman, a professor at the University of Pennsylvania . . . has a strategy for reforming a profession he thinks has gone awry. . . .

> 'Psychology,' he said, 'has been negative essentially for 100 years. Theories have generally focused on damage, as have techniques for intervention. Social science has believed negative things were authentic and strengths were coping mechanisms,' he said. . . .

> But what he sees in his (own) children are 'pure, unadulterated strengths that are not compensations for trauma, but intrinsic.' Seligman says, 'I find myself beginning to believe psychology needs to ask, what are the virtues? We need to delineate them, assess them, ask causal questions. What are the interactions? How does it grow? Let's talk of growth and questions of strength. . . .'

> 'Rather than spending $10 million on, say, phobias and fears,' he says, 'study courage.'

The point raised by Dr. Seligman is a very important one, and one we are particularly delighted to see raised within mainstream psychology circles. It is an issue that was addressed by Alan C. Walter and myself more than forty years ago in our work with champion athletes and in improving human performance generally. That work continued, and the discoveries made over the last few years by Alan Walter, in particular, demonstrate the issue raised by Dr. Seligman is now very much resolved.

Similarly, the work that Alan Walter and I have been involved in aligns with and gives greater understanding to the discoveries of Bruce Lipton, Rudolph Steiner and Maria Montessori. The discoveries and technology developed by Alan Walter are of particular and immense value here, as they explain, and provide procedures for the recovery and empowering of the true powers of you as a spiritual Being.

The *real you*, when it is recognized, honored and appreciated fully in oneself and in one's children or students, produces wondrous results.

And this is what is observed among those educators who practice the principles outlined in this chapter of:

a) recognizing the true spiritual nature of our children.

b) granting them sovereignty and self-determinism.

c) recognizing and honoring the individual's own learning style and.

d) honoring the truth that learning is a natural ability we are all gifted with and that it is to be facilitated.

I have had the pleasure to witness this at both the Waldorf and Montessori school organizations, which have been wonderful exemplars of this for seventy-five years or more. (See: www.montessori.edu and www.waldorfanswers.org)

Another organization doing very well in this regard is Bright Horizons Family Solutions (www.brighthorizons.com), which operates in most states in the U.S.

You are fortunate to have available to you the materials in this manual. I wish they had been available when I started my schooling sixty-five years ago.

This manual contains not only the fruits of nearly fifty years of research, plus a distillation of the wisdom of many of the great teachers of history, but explicitly workable answers—answers you will instantly see as correct, self evident truths based on your own experience. Best of all, it contains answers you can use!

Prepare yourself for a wondrous journey.

REHABILITATION OF CERTAINTY ON THE ABILITY TO LEARN PROCEDURE

The purpose of this procedure is to restore to the student their certainty on the truth that they can learn and that they have successfully learned in the past. The procedure will also reveal to the student the methods by which they learn.

Position:

Coach and student sitting side by side or opposite each other.

Directions:

1. Coach asks: **Recall a time you realized you successfully learned something.**
   If this does not elicit a positive response ask:
   Recall a time you were aware you had learned or accomplished something new that you wanted to do.

The answer can be anything at all the student learned or accomplished that made them competent at something. Examples could be: learning to tie their own shoe laces; learning to button their own cloths; learning to add, ride a bicycle, spell or read their first simple word, bake a cake, tie a knot.

The object of the process is to recover to the student those moments of feeling accomplished at learning or mastering something that enabled them to progress in life and be more in charge of their own affairs.

2. If student has not already told what it was ask: **What was it?**
   Acknowledge the answer* (See note below on acknowledgement).
   a) **When was that?** Acknowledge the answer.
   b) **Where was it?** Acknowledge the answer.
   c) **Describe what happened.** Acknowledge the answer.
   d) **How did it make you feel?** Acknowledge the answer.
   e) **Describe your mood level.** Acknowledge the answer.
   f) **How big were you spiritually at that time?** Acknowledge answer.
   g) **What did you do to learn** (*item learned*)? Acknowledge answer.
   h) **What did learning** (*item learned*) **enable you to do?** Ack. answer.
   i) **How have you used** (*item learned*) **to help yourself, others or another?**
      Check for more ways; acknowledge each answer.
   j) **How could you use** (*item learned*) **to help yourself, others, or another in the future?** *Check for more ways;* acknowledge each answer.
   k) **How do you feel about your ability to learn now?** Acknowledge the answer.

If student is not bright and happy about their ability to learn, repeat Steps 1 and 2, looking for the earliest time the student had a win at learning.

*By acknowledgment we mean a simple: "good," "thank you," "fine," or "OK." Do not add any opinions or other comment other than to clarify something heard in order to fully understand it. The student must be allowed to have their truth of the matter, and not have anyone else's ideas pushed onto them.

IMPORTANT NOTE

Write up any wins, insights, realizations or recovered abilities.

It is extremely important that both you and the student recognize, acknowledge, validate, honor and appreciate the wins and accomplishments of the student. Failure to correctly do so can result in the *loss of gains!* It is that important.

Refer to Appendix 6 for the reasons for this and the importance of writing up wins.

Refer to Appendix 5 for the *Futures Alignment Process* that you should use to validate, honor appreciate and empower all major wins into and for the future.

For individuals advanced or experienced in this material, the *Celebration of Regained Abilities, States and Wins Procedure* (Appendix 7) should also be used.

CHAPTER TWO

THE SEVEN BARRIERS TO COMPREHENSION THAT BLOCK LEARNING

As we said in Chapter 1, the ability to learn is a natural faculty; we are born with it. Children when young learn naturally. The big question is: What gets in its way?

Knowing this, we have discovered there are several critical issues connected to learning which, if unknown and therefore mishandled, will block any effort to arrive at full comprehension and learn what was intended. We call these *The Barriers to Comprehension*.

These are the critical errors educators and parents must ensure they do not inflict on their students. They are the critical issues all students must themselves understand so they can avoid them.

The positive side of this is that, when understood, these phenomena can be harnessed as positive enhancers in both the learning activity and in life.

These phenomena are noted below. They will each be dealt with in depth in their own chapter to follow.

1. NOT KNOWING THE PURPOSE & VALUE OF THE SUBJECT & YOUR INTENTION FOR STUDYING IT

2. PRECEPTS AND FALSE OR PRECONCEIVED NOTIONS OF WHAT IS CORRECT OR SHOULD BE

3. ABSENT DEFINITIONS AND MISUNDERSTOOD WORDS

4. BY-PASSED GRADIENTS & MISSING FOUNDATIONAL KNOWLEDGE

5. AN IMBALANCE OF THEORY VERUS ACTION OR EXPERIENTIAL KNOWLEDGE: MASS VERSUS MEANING AND SIGNIFICANCE

6. LACK OF APPRECIATION

7. FAILURE TO RECOGNIZE OR ASSIGN CORRECT AND RELATIVE ORDERS OF IMPORTANCE

These *Barriers to Comprehension and Learning* are listed in the sequence you are most likely to encounter them, not in their order of importance.

Let us now deal with each in depth.

CHAPTER THREE

LEARNING BARRIER ONE

NOT KNOWING THE PURPOSE AND VALUE OF THE SUBJECT
&
YOUR INTENTION FOR STUDYING IT

The purpose of the subject, and *your intention for studying it:* These are actually two separate and large subjects with regards study and learning, but we have combined them for the purposes of this introduction.

When a student sees no purpose for the subject he or she is being made to study, the student will do miserably with it and fail. At best, their attention will wander and not be applied to learning. At worst, the student will become destructive to the learning environment (as we see in our schools today).

Value and Applicability

As with life, students need to see a reason for paying attention to a subject; *they need to see the value or applicability of a subject to be "bothered" learning it* — particularly in this modern society with so much cramming the student's attention. If they see no purpose for, or applicability of, a subject, it has no value to them; and even if the subject truly has value the student will not give it attention and it will be wasted. Herein lays the riddle of why so many modern-day students find subjects "uninteresting," "boring," "useless," and then fail them — their educators most likely never informed them of the use, applicability, value or purpose of the subject.

As an exercise, take the subject of mathematics. Either check your own experience when learning it, or question others on their experience.

Check the aspects of mathematics you or the other person did poorly with. Did you or they see any purpose, applicability or use for that particular part of the subject? (The same exercise may be applied regarding grammar, history or any other subject.)

I know in my own case, I saw no use for algebra and all of its "stupid," illogical rules, and I did very, very poorly with it to the extent of eventually failing

16

the subject. My co-author, Virginia, saw no use for geometry, and rebelled against having to reprove theorems that already had been proved for two-thousand years, with similar failing result. Our teachers never explained the purpose or use of these subjects. History is a subject for which students commonly see no purpose and consequently find "boring" and "useless."

When Virginia and I run workshops on this material for educators (tutors and schoolteachers), and have them do the drill that follows, we find it highly entertaining to see the class melt into hilarity when they each begin to discover why they themselves did poorly or had difficulty in subjects due to this learning barrier.

The subject of *purpose* is a vitally important one, as it is the reason why one invests, or not, one's life-force, energy or attention in anything. It is indeed, a key to life.

Many famous authors and educators have written on the importance of *purpose*. Peter F. Drucker revolutionized modern management principles by causing executives to correctly delineate their corporate and divisional purposes. Authors such as Dale Carnegie, Napoleon Hill, Wallace D. Wattles and Tony Robbins saved many careers, even lives, and taught people how to be successful and acquire riches by correct delineation of *purpose*.

That is the importance of *purpose*.

Student's own Reason and Intention for Studying

Distinct from the *purpose* and *value* of the subject, is the student's *own reason for studying* it — his or her *intention* for studying the subject. This is hugely important, as it determines not only how the subject will be used, and even if it will be used, but whether it will be learned properly and in proper context.

When a student has a wrong or inapplicable intention for his or her study, the student will fail to learn the subject properly. He or she will misuse what has been "learned" of it, and will never become a master of it.

Confucius observed this even in his day. He is famous for saying, "In ancient times men studied for the sake of self-improvement; nowadays men study in order to impress other people."

The only proper and worthwhile intention one should have for studying any subject is in order *to apply what is learned in a masterful fashion for the accomplishment of worthwhile results toward an ideal.*

Positive intentions are what spark and fire-up our pursuit of purpose; our persistence on any given course to the attainment of desired results.

Too many students have wrong intentions for studying — intentions such as status, to be entertained, to pass the time, only to get a credential, because someone else wanted them to, etc. Life is too valuable to be wasted on inadequate, meaningless intentions. But worse, wrong or inapplicable intentions for the study of any subject leads to both poor results *and* disastrous consequences.

One sees this in the practice of careers. Professions that have bad reputations such as politics or law are examples of this. Ideally, law is the subject of equity and justice, and of optimum conduct of societal affairs. Yet too many lawyers have studied the subject and then used their knowledge in order to misuse the system. Hence the ill repute the profession is held in, and the damage this incorrect intention does in society.

Politics has been perverted by practitioners who, instead of conducting the affairs of office as the elected representatives for the benefit of their communities (as was their promise when being elected), conduct the affairs of their office only for their own benefit or hidden agendas.

The subject of medicine is another example. Having traveled the world and lived in many different countries enables me to make comparisons. When one compares the practice of American medicine to that of other countries, one can observe that American medicine has been corrupted by the intention "to make money" versus the intention to heal. In England and Europe, medicine is studied and practiced with the intention to heal.

There are many other specific examples that could be cited as to how the practices of other professions have been corrupted by inappropriate intentions — and it can all be simply traced back to the point that too many in these areas began and pursued their studies based on a wrong or less than ideal intention as compared to what the stated principles of the endeavor are.

Are there any examples of correctly aligned and implemented positive intentions? Yes, there are, take C-SPAN, the cable television network.

C-SPAN was founded on the bright idea and principle that a properly informed citizenry can responsibly and more correctly guide and determine its affairs. Its founder, Brian Lamb, knew that to accomplish this he would have to create a vehicle that disseminated the facts of events free from any advertising or other sponsorship influence and also free from any added opinion by the organization itself.

Brian was brilliant enough to sell the idea to the cable signal carriers, and for them to implement it as a public service.

If you watch C-SPAN closely, you'll notice none of its staff ever add any opinion to anything. Even discussing the weather during some of their events, it's never a "wonderful" day, but a "bright, sunny day." You'll notice events speak for themselves in full; presentations or speeches by newsmakers are presented in total and without any added comment by staff other than a statement of fact as to who spoke, on what, where and when. Thus the citizenry get the facts of the event only.

I always marveled that Brian Lamb's own program which he did for many years, *Booknotes*, was conducted without any dialogue from him other than to introduce and then simply ask questions of the guest author. And Brian would then to be silent while the guest answered the question in full. There was never any added comment or opinion given by Brian.

I once complimented him on his good manners and the fact that the program was so enjoyable because we got the chance to hear the author's answers without interruption or distraction. Brian chided me with the answer, "But that's because I'm actually lazy, and that's the easy way to do it." He was smiling broadly, and I knew the truth was that he was rigorously implementing the original, honest intent that founded C–SPAN and fulfilling its policy of keeping all programming free of added opinion.

Thus we see this subject of the ***intention*** for any endeavor, or study, one embarks on is a big one. It is so important, it determines not only success in learning, but prosperity and the ability to truly win in life.

Thus we have a maxim:

The only way to truly succeed in any learning endeavor (or other life activity) is to have the intention to masterfully apply what is being learned (or has been learned) toward the accomplishment of a worthwhile ideal — and this includes theoretical subjects where the only apparent application is "to think with what has been learned."

Drill One: *Understanding the Purpose of a Subject and Your Intention for Studying It*, is in the **Workbook of Exercises** in the Appendix section of this manual. You can do this drill now if you wish, or do it on your second time through this manual.

CHAPTER FOUR

LEARNING BARRIER TWO

PRECEPTS AND FALSE OR PRECONCEIVED NOTIONS OF WHAT IS CORRECT OR SHOULD BE

A good dictionary defines *precept* as:

1. a commandment or direction meant as a rule of action or conduct.
2. a rule of moral conduct; maxim.
3. a rule or direction, as for doing something technical.

It comes from the Latin *praeceptum,* to admonish, teach. It is listed as a synonym of *doctrine,* and the notes of usage state: *precept* refers to an injunction or dogma intended as a rule of action or conduct (to teach by example rather than by precept).

"Belief systems" whether based on societal beliefs or self-generated beliefs can act as precepts that prevent correct perception and learning of what is truly present to be learned.

Preconceived notions and prejudices are examples of precepts which invariably alter or color what one is attempting to learn and the way it is applied — just as they alter or predetermine the way one relates to one's environment, friends, foes or family.

Precepts, Preconceived Notions and Belief Systems Block Both Learning and Correct Performance

The tragedy of many people is that both their attempts to learn and/or correctly apply what they have learned (where learning does occur) is blocked by precepts.

The Consideration That an Area, Subject or Point of Knowledge is Already Known About

The consideration that an area, subject or point of knowledge is already known about, can be a precept and a huge barrier to the full comprehension and mastery of any subject — indeed, it actually prevents perception of the subject and thus prevents learning.

You'll have seen this yourself whenever you've tried to present some information to someone who thinks they already know all about it — their consideration that "it is already known" completely blocks their ability to receive the information and prevents them from learning what you have tried to pass on to them. Further, anything they do get of your communication is distorted by what they think they already know.

There are some variations on this, not the least of which, apart from blocking learning and full comprehension, is that your information is mis-aligned with and misunderstood in terms of what they superficially think they "know."

Folk who run this pretense of "already knowing about it" on themselves and on those who try to help them, routinely alter the new information or knowledge they should be learning by mis-identifying it as being "the same as" what they "already know," when it is not. Thereby, they fail to learn, and fail to gain full comprehension of, the new knowledge.

One of the great tragedies of modern education is that many of those who pass for being educated too often have only made very superficial contact with the subjects they claim to "know about." The consequences of their superficiality are hidden ineptitude, bluff, pretense and assertions of rightness, while harboring a secret fear of being found out on really not knowing.

False Notion Precepts

False notion precepts abound in any human culture. With the benefit of hindsight, we can now look back and smile, or perhaps wince, at some of the false notion precepts that blocked civilization and its advance to the discovery and appreciation of actual truth. "The world is flat," and "The Earth is the center of the universe," are two classics.

Even today, in science, such precepts (often called scientific paradigms) block honest inspection and appreciation of what is there to be learned. The ongoing brouhaha over "cold fusion" that began in 1993 is a case in point. A group of physicists stuck in the paradigm of nuclear fission physics resorted to name-calling and labeled as "pathological science" the discovery that platinum group metal electrodes placed in a solution of heavy water emit more energy than is needed to initiate the process.

As Max Planck, the Nobel Laureate physicist said, "In science it takes sixty, not thirty years for a new and revolutionary idea to establish itself. Not only must the old professors die off, so must their students."

A close inspection of religious or interracial wars often reveals their cause is based on the presence of false notion precepts that block harmony and understanding.

Operational Precepts

Other types of precepts that block learning are those that have been put in place by the individual to solve upsets, trauma, difficulties or other chaos in life. Thus they appear to handle difficult subjects or solve areas of life the person has to confront or operate in.

They are what we call *operational precepts.*

If you listen carefully, you will hear them uttered almost continuously by folk in everyday conversation. "I don't want to know." "I'll never understand this." "It's all too difficult." "All men (or women) are the same!" "I already know about that!" "I don't want to be involved with . . !" "It's the same as . . !"

These and many, many more are examples of operational precepts, originally adopted to solve an area of difficulty, that negatively program the minds of individuals and cause them to be unable to inspect, interface with, and understand areas of life or its various activities. Thus they block learning in any areas or subjects affected by them.

A brilliantly effective procedure, *Clean Slate Handling Learning Drill,* has been developed by Alan C. Walter that "cleans the slate" of precepts and many of these barriers to comprehension so the individual can learn in any area or subject.

By "*Clean Slate*" we mean to clean the slate (the student's mind) of the debris of earlier misunderstandings and/or false belief precepts that will prevent the student from being able to grasp and learn what is being studied. This procedure provides a clean slate onto which the student can then write the true knowledge he or she is about to learn.

The *Clean Slate Handling Learning Drill* should be used on **all** key words, phrases or concepts belonging to each subject the student is studying. All students should now clean slate the words: *study, learning, and the concept/action "studying to learn"* using the *Clean Slate Handling Learning Drill.* (A stand-alone copy for easy use of this procedure also exists in the Appendix.)

The *Clean Slate Handling Learning Drill* is one of the procedures Alan developed that can be used to clear away almost all impediments to your ability to perform in any area of activity. The version we have included, next following in this chapter, is the one to use when studying. (A copy of this procedure also exists in the Appendix.) Indeed, we highly recommend the book *Creating Your New Futures Holistic Workbook* by Alan C. Walter, which delineates a procedure and approach to optimizing one's abilities and activities in life, based on the technology and principles connected to the *Clean Slate Procedure*. The companion book, *The Paradigm Matrix*, is also highly recommended. (Available from http://www.knowledgism.com or http://wisdompublishing.com)

In the **Workbook of Exercises** in the Appendix section of this manual is Drill Two, which is designed to give you additional subjective reality of how precepts can interfere with learning.

> *The beginning of wisdom is the definition of terms.*
> Socrates (470 - 399 BC)

CLEAN SLATE HANDLING LEARNING DRILL

Definitions:

YOU: The Spiritual Being; the life-force; the energizer.

TERM: *n.* 1. A word having a precise meaning. 2. Any word or phrase used in a definite or precise sense. Synonyms: word, vocable, phrase, locution, expression

WORD: *n.* 1. A sound or a combination of sounds, or its representation in writing or printing, that symbolizes and communicates a meaning. 2. Something that is said; an utterance, remark, or comment.

VOCABLE: *n.* A word considered only as a sequence of sounds or letters rather than as a unit of meaning.

PHRASE: *n.* 1. Any sequence of words intended to have meaning. 2. A word or group of words read or spoken as a unit and separated by pauses or other junctures.

LOCUTION: *n.* A particular word, phrase, or expression considered from the point of view of style.

EXPRESSION: *n.* 1. The act of expressing, conveying or representing in words, art, music, or movement; manifestation. 2. That which symbolizes something; a symbol; a sign; a token.

PRECEPT: *n.* 1. A prescribed rule of conduct or action; instruction or direction.

2. Instruction or direction regarding a given course of action, especially a maxim in morals. The basis and source of a belief system.

BELIEF SYSTEM: A belief system is the set of a person's interrelated ideas, principles, precepts, rules, or laws that governs their acceptance or conviction in the actuality of something they perceive. It is the person's mindset. Belief systems are created by the person's knowledge and experiences.

Important Note: At all times, the student should define any terms that are not fully comprehended by looking them up in the dictionary or referring to the definitions given in this book before going on.

One person reads a paragraph of the material being studied or describes the area or subject (breaking it down into its parts) to be cleaned. The other person then addresses the term, paragraph, area or subject part by asking:

1. **What is your comprehension of this?**

   Have the person look inward at their concepts, visions or models for their answer and tell you what they experience. If they present a clean, precise comprehension with certainty, go to Step 2. If they encounter confusion, pain, a gap of blackness or stupidity, have them go to a dictionary and get the terms defined. When they have a clean vision, concept or comprehension, acknowledge them and ask:

2. **Does that trigger or remind you of anything?**

   Have the person look inward for the answer.

   Tell me your perceptions about that.

   Acknowledge their answer.

3. **What precepts, beliefs or thoughts do you have about or from (*thing, area, subject, word or term being addressed*)?**

   Get the person to look inward for the answer and to tell you the precept, belief or thought. By asking the person to look inward, you are directing their attention to their comprehension, visions, concepts or mind. Acknowledge their answer.

   a. **Connected to (*named precept/belief/thought*), where is it?**

      Acknowledge their answer.

   b. **Connected to (*named precept/belief/thought*), what is its size?**

      Acknowledge their answer.

   c. **Connected to (*named precept/belief/thought*), what is its form or shape?**

      Acknowledge their answer.

   d. **Connected to (*named precept/belief/thought*), what is its color?**

      Acknowledge their answer.

   e. **Connected to (*named precept/belief/thought*), what is its weight?**

      Acknowledge their answer.

   f. **Connected to (*named precept/belief/thought*), what is its duration?**

      Acknowledge their answer.

   g. **Connected to (*named precept/belief/thought*), what are its mood levels?**

      Acknowledge their answer.

   h. **Connected to (*named precept/belief/thought*), what are its limitations?**

      Acknowledge their answer.

   i. **Connected to (*named precept/belief/thought*), what must not be experienced?**

      Acknowledge their answer.

   j. **Connected to (*named precept/belief/thought*), what must be experienced?**

Acknowledge their answer.

4. **Does (*named precept/belief/thought*) create an image or vision?** *If "Yes," say:*

    Tell me about it.

5. **How does (*named precept/belief/thought*) manifest in your presence-time?**

6a. **What have been or could be the consequences of having that precept/belief/thought?**

    Acknowledge their answer.

6b. **Have there been or could there be any other consequences?**

    Acknowledge their answer.

    Repeat Step 6b until all consequences have been viewed.

7. **Do you have any other precepts, beliefs or thoughts about or from (*thing, area, subject, word, etc., being addressed*)?**

    Repeat questions 4 to 7 until all precepts on the thing being addressed have been viewed. Then have the person reread the paragraph of the material being studied, or describe the area or subject (breaking it down into its parts) being cleaned, and ask:

8. **Connected to (*thing, area, subject, word, etc., being addressed*) do you have any misdefined terms?**

    Get the terms and fully define them in the dictionary. Repeat #8 until all misdefined terms have been found and fully comprehended, then ask:

9. **What would be the consequences of having the ability to (*whatever the ability would be for thing, area, subject, word, etc., being addressed*)?**

    Acknowledge their answer.

10. **What dream or goal does comprehending (*thing, area, subject, word, etc., being addressed*) contribute to or support?**

    Have them tell you about it and acknowledge their answer.

11. **What problem does comprehending (*thing, area, subject, word, etc., being addressed*) solve?**

    Have them tell you about it and acknowledge their answer.

12. **What vision does comprehending (*thing, area, subject, word, etc., being addressed*) create or reinforce?**

    Have them tell you about it and acknowledge their answer.

15 May 1987   ALAN C. WALTER
Revised 13 April 2005
By Roger E. Boswarva

CHAPTER FIVE

LEARNING BARRIER THREE

ABSENT DEFINITIONS AND MISUNDERSTOOD WORDS

Before you read this chapter on Learning Barrier Three: *Absent Definitions and Misunderstood Words,* we are going to have you do a little drill in order that you can experience the effect of this barrier to comprehension. This barrier has a devastating effect on both learning and one's ability to act or perform in any area or activity in life. It is a primary cause of student failure, and of failure in life. Indeed, in the presence of the non-comprehension of words, terms or symbols, a person becomes immobile and unable to act or perform. At the instant of colliding with such non-comprehension a person goes mentally blank and is less aware.

This statement is so important, we will restate it in more succinct terms.

IN THE PRESENCE OF
NON-DEFINED OR INCORRECTLY DEFINED
WORDS OR TERMS,
A PERSON IS EITHER UNABLE TO PERFORM
OR, IF FORCED TO ACT, WILL LIKELY DO SO *INCORRECTLY*

******

This is a big statement. And one that is so important that we are going to have you do a drill so you can actually experience the truth of it.

Ideally, you should get yourself a partner to do the drill. You do the drill taking turns, switching roles, so that each has the experience of acting as the coach while the other is the student. Otherwise, you can do this drill by yourself, though the experience may not be quite as startling.

DRILL THREE
RECOGNIZING NON-COMPREHENSIONS

Purpose: To give the student a subjective reality of the fact that in the presence of incompletely defined, non-defined or misunderstood words, terms and symbols, a person goes mentally blank, immobile and is unable to perform, and if forced to act, will likely do so in error.

Position Student and coach seated together or opposite each other with a good big dictionary (do not use a pocket dictionary, they miss too much).

Directions **Step 1:**
Coach commands the student to do one of the following actions (each are to choose different phrases):
a) **Demonstrate to me the concept "When crepuscule came the children ran inside."**
b) **Demonstrate to me the concept "When crepitating began the children became afraid."**
c) **Demonstrate to me the concept "When the children found the creodont they were rewarded."**

If the student at all pauses, stalls, or is otherwise non-performing or gone mentally blank, the coach is to say, "**I notice you are not performing. What is the word you don't have a clear definition for?**" Coach is to then have student consult the dictionary and obtain a full comprehension of the word(s). Don't be surprised at which words the student doesn't clearly understand and has to look up. Then the coach again commands the student to perform the incomplete demonstration. (Anything in the environment may be used in the demonstration, including a collection of small items such as paper-clips, pencils, rubber-bands, matches, etc. These items can be made to represent the parts or people and actions in the demonstration)

Step 2:
Ask Student: **Did anything trigger or come to mind while doing this drill?**
If so, say: **Tell me about it.** Acknowledge the answer with "OK" or "Thank you." Do not make any further comment, only acknowledge.

Write up any wins, insights or cognitions.

Coach and student now switch roles, using a different phrase to demonstrate.

LEARNING BARRIER THREE

ABSENT DEFINITIONS AND MISUNDERSTOOD WORDS, TERMS & SYMBOLS

Words, terms or symbols for which you have absent definitions and/or misunderstood definitions. This is a hugely important item, *critically* important. Language is a system of symbols that represent concepts and/or objects, and the symbols can be expressed in sound, written form or other means (for example: semaphore, dance or even electronic blips). Note also that mathematics is expressed by use of its own system of symbols. If you don't have accurate and applicable definitions for the words, terms, symbols, gestures or sounds being used, you are going to be plagued with misunderstandings and non-comprehension. It's a guaranteed path to failure in life.

At this juncture, we hope you have a clear understanding of the meaning of the following words: *word, term, symbol.* If not, you must consult a good big dictionary so as to obtain the needed comprehension to benefit from this very important chapter.

Most people don't use dictionaries as much as they should. Dictionaries are not even a staple in schools, and teachers often don't define new words, terms, or symbols when they are used. The great trap is that people *invent* definitions for unknown or vaguely understood words when they come across them while reading. They don't reach for a dictionary and get it *right*; they sabotage themselves by assuming what the meaning is based on the sentence in which it is used. Then they wonder why they don't learn, feel dull, drowsy and fall asleep, or get maniacally "hyper" while studying!

It is thus critically important that parents and teachers define all new words, terms and symbols *when they are first introduced to the student. It is essential that no student be left with any non-defined, non-understood or misunderstood words, terms or symbols as they progress through their studies. To allow this, or cause it, is to sabotage the child. It is that serious an issue.*

The Reason for Failed Subjects

Here is a little exercise you can carry out to test this principle that in the presence of non-defined words, terms or symbols an individual is unable to perform.

Check your own experience, or that of your friends, on subjects you or they did poorly with. Examples: algebra, geometry, grammar, trigonometry, etc. Ask them if they can give you the definition of the word that is the name of the subject (example: algebra). In all probability, the word was never defined when it was first introduced to them, and ever after, that subject was an area of non-comprehension for them.

There are several phenomena associated with non-understood and misunderstood words or symbols, and they produce physical symptoms.

The first thing to know is that when you go past a word or symbol for which you do not have a definition, you will go mentally blank. It's subtle, but you'll run into non-comprehension, and the passage you read immediately after the non-comprehension will be blank to you. If you were to later be given a test on what you read, that material immediately after the non-understood, non-comprehension would not be there for you; it would be blank. In fact, we find we can recover an individual's past education and restore knowledge to him or her simply by locating all the non-defined, absent-definition words encountered during his or her study on any subject.

This is true, also, for words individuals think they know but only have partial definitions for. This is because the *missing* definition may have been the sense or usage in which the word was meant, and it acts as a non-defined word. It is also true that such incompletely defined words can cause misunderstanding. This is because the definition and sense of the word the individual knows is not the correct one for the passage or sentence in which it was used, so his or her use of the incorrect sense or meaning of the word causes them to grossly misunderstand what was intended by the material they just read or heard.

So to repeat: **This is such a powerfully crippling mechanism, that in the presence of a non-understood word (absent definition) or an incompletely understood word, the blankness and non-comprehension can be so damning that an individual is stopped, unable to act or perform. He or she is at a complete loss, made numb and immobile.** If you doubt the power of this, recall the last time you could not act or perform, locate what the non-understood/non-comprehension was, define all the words involved — and then see how you do!

Wrong definitions do the same thing to the individual, but with the added twist that wrong definitions (misunderstood and wrongly understood words) give you erroneous understandings of what you read or hear. You simply get things wrong, and act stupidly and incompetently.

Going mentally blank is the immediate symptom you experience when you collide with a non-defined word. The other mental and physical symptoms you will experience when you *go on past* non-understoods, partially understoods or misunderstoods and try to continue is a drowsiness, a loss of awareness, a fog in the mind. You'll begin to yawn, even begin to dope off. Now you know how it is that people read themselves to sleep! When you accumulate too many non-comprehended words on a subject, you eventually abandon it! (There are technical phenomena behind why this occurs, which is discussed elsewhere in our materials.)

Technically, you can trace much of an individual's inability and much of his or her stupidity, confused notions and confused thinking to this subject of absent definitions and misunderstood words, terms and symbols. And you can remedy their ability and intelligence by addressing it.

Non-understood words and misunderstood words are a primary "why" for the dullness you experience in life. And they are the reason you *abandoned* the subjects you tried to learn but failed. Now is your chance to clean that up!

Don't sabotage yourself. Use a good dictionary.

Misunderstood Versus Non-Understood or Not Understood

There is a distinction between a *mis*understood and a *non*-understood word. If you didn't spot the difference when you first read the beginning of this chapter (and many people think they are "sort-of-the-same" when they first see them), now is the time for you to do your next drill of this course! You need to clearly understand the difference between a *non*-understood and a *mis*understood. (The drill is written at the end of this chapter and also in the **Workbook of Exercises** in the Appendix as Drill Four.)

And now is the time to do it, not later. There is a reason for this, as you will see later. We are interested in you becoming competent, not staying incompetent!

The reason a misunderstood and a non-understood word appear to be the same to most folk is because they routinely turn their non-understood words into misunderstood words as a result of inventing definitions for non-understood words when they first encounter them. Routinely, the sequence is that the person comes across a word while reading, or even while listening to another, that they don't clearly know the meaning of and, instead of reaching for a dictionary or otherwise getting the word defined, they invent or assume a meaning based on the context of what they are reading. These invented definitions are invariably off the mark, inadequate and erroneous. And so they sabotage themselves.

Now you have the key to why it is some of those dullards you collide with never seem to get simple instructions or communications when you give them, or folk sometimes seem to get totally "off the wall" concepts of what it is you are saying to them. It is because they don't understand. They have and are operating on misunderstoods; they have invented or erroneous definitions given them by others or invented by themselves; or they have incomplete or absent definitions. So they can't comprehend, and can't think correctly.

As I said, this is an important subject. It is so important that the crashing of American educational standards can primarily be traced to its violation. Here is how it happened.

Knocked-Out Basics

The letters of the alphabet are symbols, as are punctuation marks, and unless it is clearly understood by students what they mean and represent, comprehension during the schooling of our children can't take place. Many kids today are actually not taught that those symbols called the letters of the alphabet represent sounds, nor what sounds each represents. They are no longer taught the phonetic alphabet. They have never learned that the letter "a" represents several different sounds. They don't even know that the alphabet is a system of symbols that represent sounds — yet the alphabet and the sounds it represents is the basis of any written language!

When I was in school during the 1940's and early 1950's in Australia, everyone could read. We had a workable system of teaching based on getting the basics understood. Today, American schools have knocked out the workable system, and the basics, and replaced it with "modern methods" that have produced ninety percent illiteracy rates in some geographic areas and around thirty percent "functional illiteracy rate" nationally.

As noted in *"The Importance of This Book & Manual"* section at the front of this manual, the 2003 Department of Education's National Assessment of Adult Literacy found that even among college graduates, sixty-nine percent could not read at a competent level. So you see, this *is* an important subject for those whose intention it is to be competent and masterly in all they study.

A True Story

As an example of the applicability and value of this datum, let me tell you a story about a lady I was once asked to coach. She was having trouble using a particular diagnostic tool, even though she had done the training course for its use *twice*, and "passed" both times as competent.

On watching her do the drills for the operation of the instrument, I observed she manifested the symptoms of a by-passed gradient (as discussed in the next chapter). Picking this up, I took her back to the earlier gradient step of learning to do a subsidiary action in the use of the equipment.

While doing that earlier training step, I observed she manifested the symptoms of a non-comprehension. Something was either *not* understood or it was *mis*understood, and it had to be in the written instructions she had read. Even though she bluffed her way forward, gamely pressing on, it was clear to me she had not understood something as she should have.

I had her read aloud to me those instructions while I watched for the manifestations of the misunderstood or not-understood (as in absence of understanding due to a missing definition) that I knew would turn on while she read the material. As she read the material, I observed she went past the *commas* without expressing them by way of pause or change of intonation that signifies the presence of a comma and the change of thought they often introduce. She actually behaved as though the commas were not there. In fact I observed her go blank as she passed over each comma.

At that point I stopped her and asked, "What is the definition of a comma?" "It means *and*," she replied.

"Let's look it up in the dictionary," said I.

It was a major revelation to her. All her life, since being a girl of seven or eight when a schoolteacher told her "Commas mean '*and*,' as in apples, oranges, bananas" (*which they **don't***), she never factually got the true meaning of any sentence that carried a comma! Floods of tears and emotion erupted as she *now* saw the reason why she had had so much difficulty in getting some things straight that she'd read. She wasn't dumb after all! She'd been misled by her teacher by being given a misunderstanding, by way of a false definition!

After a break for her to calm down and have the win of the discovery, we continued on with the exercise. *Now* she read the instructions with new understanding — and it was real understanding and full comprehension. She then completed the practical drill section of the exercise brilliantly.

I've seen my friend from time to time in the twenty years since then. She tells me getting the correct definition of what a comma is saved her career. But for me it is nicer to see that she is now so much happier, winning in life, no longer erroneously thinking she is dumb or dull.

That's the magic of this particular piece of technology. Use it!

And by the way, it's not just we regular folk who misunderstand these punctuation symbols. When I lived in England, I saw major brouhahas in the courts and in Parliament over the usage, placement and meaning of punctuation. In Parliament it was because it affected the meaning of legislation when written. In the courts it was the result of suits brought over contract disputes, though on one occasion it was the Inland Revenue Service suing a taxpayer based on a disagreement over what the placement and meaning of a comma was.

Indeed, such a contract dispute will likely cost Canada's largest cable television provider, Rogers Communications, $1,000,000 (Canadian) because, in October 2006, the courts found its lawyers' interpretation of a comma to be incorrect (though the case is on appeal as we write).

Punctuation is Important

Punctuation is extremely important, and its usage exact. You totally change the meaning of a sentence by use of punctuation.

Look at the example below. The exact same words are used in the exact same sequence, yet the meanings of the sentences are changed by the use punctuation.

> A woman, without her man, is nothing.
> A woman: without her, man is nothing.

See how important punctuation is? See how important it is you understand what each punctuation mark or symbol means?

School Drop-Outs

As we mention above, non-understood words, non-comprehended terms, symbols and actions, and misunderstood words, terms, symbols and actions are the primary underlying reason for abandonment of study.

The student feels stupid and dull, and simply drops out. And it is a huge problem in today's schools.

A November 20, 2006, *ABC News* headline read, "Students Dropping Out of High School Reaches Epidemic Levels."

The news piece went on to say, "In several of the largest school systems across the country—from Baltimore to Cleveland to Atlanta to Oakland, CA—half the students are dropping out." It then went on to cite the recent Department of Education study that found thirty-one percent of students were dropping out or failing to graduate in the nation's largest 100 public school districts.

Yet the remedy is a simple one. Do not abuse students with the use of words, terms, symbols or actions that are not defined or explained! Employ liberal use of good dictionaries.

And it must be noted that this practice has to be in place at the *beginning* of the child's schooling and continue throughout its education.

***

WORD COMPREHENSION
HOW TO LEARN DEFINITIONS FROM A DICTIONARY

Most folk have never been taught how to use a dictionary, and most have certainly not read the "Guide to the Use of the Dictionary" which comprises the first section of every dictionary. Maybe this is symptomatic of a culture that believes it learns everything by some sort of magical osmosis. Either way, it is very instructive to learn how your dictionary has been structured, why it has been presented in the way it has, how it works, and what all those funny abbreviations mean.

But that is not the purpose of this particular section. It is about how you go about obtaining a clear comprehension of word definitions from a dictionary.

What you should ideally strive for when obtaining definitions of words and terms from a dictionary is a holographic conceptual understanding. This is a level of understanding wherein your usage of the word and concept it represents is facile and instantly known. The knowledge the word represents is then not something you have to think about. It is instantly available, and your use of it blossoms holographically without any mental fuzz.

It is not uncommon for students to collide with difficulty or "mental fuzz" when they are trying to obtain full comprehension of definitions by use of a dictionary. There are several reasons and remedies for this.

The first thing to know is that any new knowledge you attempt to gain will be compared against, aligned relative to, classified and filed in your "mind" according to your past experience and the things you already are familiar with. This can have the liability that it triggers earlier material that may contain unpleasant sensations, pain, non-comprehension, chronic moods or misunderstoods.

Generally, the remedy for this is to repeat the action that triggered the earlier similar experience. Simply continue, by repeating the action of confronting the word and its definitions, and *applying the word in several sentences* — being sure to use *each* of the senses defined in the dictionary — *until you know you have a clear grasp and conceptual understanding of the word and its meanings and can use it.*

You do this by simply creating numbers of sentences that use the word and saying them to yourself or your study partner. You'll find as you do this, the mental fuzz will blow off.

Ideally, you should obtain a three-dimensional holographic comprehension of the concept being defined.

You will find, sometimes, that you will need to consult more than one dictionary — sometimes several, including special technical dictionaries. That's the only honest way to learn words to full comprehension. You do whatever it takes to get the full comprehension you need. The reason you will sometimes need to consult different dictionaries, apart from special technical dictionaries, is that even among supposedly "standard" dictionaries, definitions differ. And they differ in two main respects:

a) Some dictionary publishers consider themselves to be progressive (they change definitions as usage of the word in society changes), while others stick to and maintain the standards that are historically accurate.

b) Some dictionaries are very clear in their definitions, and some are not.

- If you go to the 1945 edition of the C. & C. Merriam Company's *Webster's Collegiate Dictionary: Fifth Edition*, you will find an *incorrect* definition for the word "entropy," which is correctly defined at the end of this sub-paragraph.

- If you go to Merriam's 1981 edition of their *Webster's New Collegiate Dictionary*, you will find an incomprehensible definition that is so abstruse it is hard to know if it is in error or not (and I'm not joking, it is actually that bad).

- Going to *The Merriam-Webster Home and Office Edition* (1995), you find a grossly incomplete definition that is so deficient that it actually *omits* the main, basic and primary meaning of the word and, using only secondary lesser important definitions expressed in inadequate sound-bite language (one of which is their own invented definition), it will completely mislead any student.

The **Definition of Entropy** in the 1958 *Webster's New World Dictionary of the American Language: College Edition,* by The World Publishing Company, which is elegant and precise is: "in *physics,* the theoretical measure of energy, as of steam, which cannot be transformed into mechanical work in a thermodynamic system." Their Second College Edition, published in 1970, still elegant and precise, expands the number of senses defined.

Thus, you will benefit from consulting several dictionaries — and you should use a big dictionary, not one of those abbreviated or pocket editions. You miss too much if you use a small one.

Be sure you define all new words and symbols as you come across them *within* the definition of the word you are clearing.

Sometimes defining words in dictionaries exposes the student to a lot of theory or significance, and this induces an imbalance between that theory and the action or masses connected to the subject (See Chapter 8, *Learning Barrier Five: An Imbalance of Action and Theory or Mass and Significance).* Remedy this by doing a little of the action involved or by drawing a diagram or getting some odds and ends (pins, paper clips, rubber bands, etc.) that can be made to represent various items connected to the word, subject or definition and *demonstrate* the meaning. Also you can get a picture of the object that is being defined. Good dictionaries often give you pictures.

All these actions can help you get a clear comprehension of the meaning and use of a word. As with the mental fuzz above, you'll observe the evaporation of that heavy, massy, squashed and crushed feeling you were experiencing due to the imbalance of theory to mass/action when you introduce the mass or action. It's quite magical!

Occasionally, you can get hung up in trying to take a word to full comprehension because you have an *earlier* false definition, or an *earlier* invented definition (that is false) getting in the way. You keep trying to put this new correct meaning into your head, and it just won't go in!

When you are well versed in all this, you simply have a look, spot the earlier goofy definition(s) that's in the way and delete it as incorrect. Failing this, the thing to do is the *Clean Slate Handling Learning Drill.*

Clean Slating is the proven method of handling things that get in the way of learning, or masterly performance. It should be used on all key concepts and critical areas of knowledge and skills.

Drill Number Four in the *Workbook of Exercises* in the Appendix may be done now or on your second reading of this manual. Its purpose is to give you a subjective reality of how freeing it is to clarify incompletely understood or misunderstood words or terms.

DRILL FOUR
CLARIFYING MISUNDERSTOOD & ABSENT DEFINITIONS

Purpose of the Exercise: To give the student a subjective reality of how freeing it is to clarify incompletely understood or misunderstood words or terms.

Part One
Write down your current understanding of:

Prefix:

_____
_____
_____
_____

Mis:

_____
_____
_____
_____

Non:

_____
_____
_____
_____

Look up these words in a good dictionary and write down their definitions.

Prefix:

_____
_____
_____
_____

Mis:

_____
_____
_____
_____

Non:

_____

_____

_____

_____

How does your definition compare to or differ from the dictionary definition?

If the definitions were quite different, can you spot when, where and from whom you received your definition? Did you invent your own definition in the place of and due to the absence of the correct definition?

Remove any incorrect definition from your mind and replace it with the correct dictionary definition (if this has not already happened).

Write up any wins, insights or cognitions.

Part Two
    a) Doing this drill may have triggered or called to mind times you went past an incompletely understood, non-understood or misunderstood word or symbol.
    b) If so, write down each such word or symbol.
    c) Using a good dictionary, define each such word or symbol.
    d) When you have the opportunity, re-read the material where you earlier went past these non-understood words or symbols and recover the knowledge.
    e) While it may take some time, it is a very fruitful exercise to address the subjects that are important to you to erase all non-comprehensions caused by non-defined, incompletely defined or misunderstood words, terms or symbols. You will recover a vast amount of clarity and intelligence.

Write up any wins, insights or cognitions.

CHAPTER SIX

LEARNING BARRIER FOUR

BY-PASSED GRADIENTS & MISSING FOUNDATIONAL KNOWLEDGE

By-passed, missed, or skimped gradients and/or foundational knowledge are the next cause of failure to learn. Usually, this is due to errors by educators, teachers and coaches, but you can do it to yourself as well. The learning of any subject or skill requires the correct sequence of knowledge acquisition or skill development. Subsequent, **higher levels of knowledge can only be aligned and comprehended when earlier basics and gradients of information or knowledge are in possession of the individual.**

The story I related in *"The Importance of This Book & Manual"* section at the beginning of this book, regarding what happened in my sister's early schooling is, of course, a tragic, true example of what happens when learning gradients are by-passed, dropped out or missed.

In the case of performance skills, higher-level mastery requires you learn and develop the basic, component skills first, then learn to combine the use of these basics into a higher level of operation or, once a lower level of operation is mastered, to *then* increase the level of difficulty.

Examples of this abound. Imagine, as a beginner, attempting to learn to ski (and I have taught many friends to ski) and being given a pair of high-powered racing skis and put on the top of the most difficult expert-only run for your first attempt to ski. Of course it's crazy! It's too steep a gradient. You know the right way to go about it is to start out gently.

The right way to learn to ski is to start out with a very short pair of skis — this way you get a chance to learn how to manipulate the skis, to turn them, to stop and such, without being given too many losses and getting totally frustrated (not to say injured) and giving up on this crazy sport. You would also start out on an appropriately gentle slope that you could manage and win at. Next you would go to a steeper slope, then a more steep one, and so on. Also, as you master the mechanics of turning your short skis, you would then increase the length of your skis a couple of times till eventually you were using the ideal skis for your height, weight and desired skill level. That way learning becomes fun and is effective. By-pass a gradient anywhere along the line and you will have losses and end up exasperated.

This is true for *all* learning endeavors.

When I teach folk to swim, the very first gradient I put in for them is the fact that if they take a full, deep breath and hold it while keeping every part of the body from the neck down below the water, they cannot sink; they will simply float at the top of the water where they can continue to snatch breaths of air. The next thing to teach is how to use their hands under the water to give their body lift, and so on.

Take mathematics. You would never learn how to do square roots without first learning the multiplication tables, then learn how to divide, then learn long division, and then take on square roots.

Take learning to read and write. There is a correct sequence of gradient steps that must be part of the process of learning to read. First is learning that those symbols of the alphabet represent sounds. Next is learning what sounds each represent. Then learning how the sounds relate to each other in forming words. Then learning the compound sounds formed by groups of letters. Then learning how these parts can be put together to form words comprising more than one syllable.

All Subjects Must be Broken Down into Their Correct Gradients of Approach for Learning

This is why an educator or parent who knows the material in this book would carefully structure the courses, or sequence of subject matter or skills to be learned, to ensure the correct gradient of learning, discovery, and skills development for the student or child. *All* subjects can and should be broken down into their correct gradients of approach for learning.

Anytime you address a subject, skill or ability you want to learn, or teach, be alert to this — be sure to first break it down into the gradient steps that should be learned, and approach them in the right order. Equally important, be ever alert to the symptoms (as below) of the by-passed gradient when they manifest so you can backtrack and get it right.

Great masters of any activity do this. They achieve their mastery by having broken down the subject of their area of mastery into its parts and practice, practice, practice each of those parts until mastered. Then they combine the parts into the whole of the performance.

This subject of by-passed gradients also has a subtle twist to it — you can *give yourself* a by-passed gradient by skimping and failing to learn properly a step that *was* provided to you. If you fail to learn the early material properly or fail to develop the proper early level of skill required, when you go to the *next* level of study or skill development, you will *at that time at the higher gradient* begin to have trouble — *real* trouble.

It must be noted, also, that students can be given by-passed gradients by teachers or instructors *going too fast*.

I well remember a mathematics class when I was a boy in which this happened. The teacher knew what he was doing, of course. It was all clear to him! But he failed miserably to pass that knowledge on to most of the lads in his class. With back to his class, our wizard teacher spoke his brilliance while writing out the sequence of functions in the operations of the equations he was trying to convey to us. Snap and pop! It was all brilliant and fast — *too* fast.

I and most of the class could not follow it. The teacher failed to pause to explain the new elements being introduced during the lesson. What we were supposed to have been learning were some new functions and operations, and the symbols and notation used to express them.

Of course, mathematical calculation is a logic sequence, and unless the student can follow each step of the logic sequence, they are lost. The easiest way to lose your student is to go too fast and to fail to define or explain the new terms introduced!

Learning and comprehension of new knowledge, skills or abilities requires that the new and unfamiliar be compared to and aligned with the familiar of the knowledge or ability already in possession of the student. When the new information is being relayed too fast for the student to assimilate, align and relate, this vital step is knocked out, and it acts as a by-passed gradient because the new knowledge is not fully assimilated.

Thus by-passed gradients can result from omitted steps or knowledge, skimping on steps of knowledge or skills acquisition, missing steps or knowledge, going too fast and not allowing correct alignment of new knowledge.

An Important Ability is the Ability to Recognize When You Have By-passed a Gradient While You Are Attempting to Learn

And here is the big point about by-passed gradients: It's *not* the step or gradient you appear to be having trouble with that is the trouble — it is an *earlier* step or gradient that you missed either because it wasn't there or wasn't presented, or you skimped on it or failed to get it aligned or done properly.

Therefore, the remedy for handling any action you are having real difficulty with is to go back and find the by-passed gradient, the skimped or not properly gotten *prior* step, and remedy *that* one. Then you'll be able to succeed with the one you are having difficulty with. It's rather magical.

Remember, it's a *by-passed* gradient — *go back*, and get it!

How to Recognize a By-passed Gradient or Missing Foundational Basic Knowledge

There are physical and mental symptoms associated with by-passing a gradient. You'll experience them when you attempt the *next* step or one very soon *after* the one missed or not properly gotten. When you by-pass a gradient and go on to what is now too steep a gradient, you'll feel suddenly confused; a reeling confusion will turn on throughout your awareness. You can also feel a sickening emptiness in the stomach or as though you are dispersing — you are there, but you feel as though you are dispersing, not able to focus and concentrate. That's the time to recognize the by-passed gradient, before you get into too much trouble. Go back and find the missed step and get it in.

Here is a drill you can do in order to experience the phenomena associated with by-passing a gradient.

DRILL FIVE
PART ONE

RECOGNIZING BY-PASSED GRADIENTS

Purpose: To give the student a subjective reality of what happens when a study or learning gradient is missed.

Position: Student and coach seated together or opposite each other with a pad of paper and pen, pencil or even a calculator.

Directions: **Step 1**
Coach commands the student to do the following action:
Perform the following sequence of calculations in your mind: 2 times 2 are 4, 2 times 4 are 8, 2 times 8 are 16 and continue multiplying the product of each multiplication again by two as far as you can go mentally until you lose control of the calculation.

Coach waits until the student reaches his or her point of confusion or lost control of ability to continue mentally calculating. When the student indicates he or she has reached the point of lost control, acknowledge and say the following: **Now take the pen and paper and, in writing, repeat the last two calculations you had control of and continue the sequence of calculations two levels past where you just stopped.**

When the student has done so, ask: **What did you notice happen?**

Acknowledge his or her answer.

Step 2
Ask Student: **Did anything trigger or come to mind while doing this drill?**
If so, say: **Tell me about it.** Acknowledge the answer with "OK" or "Thank you." Do not make any further comment, only acknowledge.

Note this drill also employs the principle of introducing a mass or physical action to balance the thought and significance process (See *Learning Barrier Five* in Chapter 7).

Write up any wins, insights or cognitions.

DRILL FIVE
PART TWO

HANDLING BY-PASSED GRADIENTS

Purpose: 1) To handle any by-passed gradients that may have been triggered or called to mind while studying the forgoing chapter or doing Part One of this drill; 2) to give the student a subjective reality of what happens when a missed study or learning gradient is corrected.

Position: Coach and student seated comfortably together or opposite each other.

Directions:
    Step 1. Coach asks the student: **While reading this chapter or doing the drill, did any past study confusion, inability to perform or by-passed gradient get triggered or come to view?** If so:
        a) Ask student, **When was that earlier confusion, inability to perform or by-passed gradient?** Acknowledge answer.
        b) **Where did it occur?** Acknowledge answer.
        c) **What was the subject you were studying?** Acknowledge answer.
        d) Ask the student to, *Go earlier in the study of that subject to when you were doing well.* Have the student let you know when they are there.
        e) Have the student address and demonstrate competence of that earlier winning point. Acknowledge it when done.
        f) Now trace forward to the next step or action of study in that past course and help the student master it. Apply any and all of the actions

noted in this manual, as needed, to help the student master this earlier missed gradient. It is possible the missed gradient was never even presented to the student for study or practice; discovering this might have to be part of the debugging process.

Going past a non-defined word or having a misunderstood word are examples of other barriers to comprehension that could be the cause of a by-passing of a gradient. It is to be noted that the step the student is stuck on or having difficulty with is *not* the by-passed gradient. The by-passed gradient is earlier at a lower learning or study level, and it is this which is the cause of the student having difficulty at the higher, later level.

g) Have the student restudy and learn to a level of competence the later material(s) or action(s) that followed the by-passed gradient; that is, the material or actions where difficulty manifested due to the earlier by-passed gradient.

Step 2.

Ask Student: **Did anything trigger or come to mind while doing this drill?**

If so, say: **Tell me about it.** Acknowledge the answer with "OK" or "Thank you." Do not make any further comment, only acknowledge.

Write up any wins, cognitions or insights.

CHAPTER SEVEN

LEARNING BARRIER FIVE

AN IMBALANCE OF THEORY VERUS ACTION OR EXPERIENTIAL KNOWLEDGE: MASS VERSUS MEANING AND SIGNIFICANCE

A proper balance and relationship between theoretical knowledge and practical or real world experience is essential to optimum learning. This requires a correct balance between the action elements of a subject and its theory, or the mass of a subject and its significance elements.

Imagine trying to learn to ride a horse simply by reading a book and not going near a horse. You could then claim to know *about* riding a horse, but certainly not to have *learned to ride* a horse. You would also have a very tough time mentally, as you would suffer the physical/mental symptoms (explained below) of the imbalance of the theory to action, and the imbalance of the missing mass (of no horse) versus the amount of significance (all the theory about it).

Take the example of learning to ski. All the ski-instructors I've ever met only keep telling you *what* to do, and *how* to do it — but never *why* you do it. They never tell you the *significance* of the action.

You, the poor student, keep trying to do it like the instructor says, but somehow or other it's tough and it keeps going wrong and you can't figure out why. (Notice here, that as you get exasperated, you begin to attempt to get some "whys" — some significance, some explanation, some theory and meaning in order to balance all this difficult [and failing] action!)

Absence of Needed Theory & Significance

The problem is that ski instructors never tell you *why* and *how* a ski turns; why the ski is designed the way it is — yet, when this simple piece of *theory* is given to skiing students (as I always do), suddenly, magically, all becomes simple; all goes right, and understanding and success become the fun of the day.

The Use of Theory & Significance

And that piece of theory? Skis are hour-glass shaped, with the back being narrower than the front; thus, when you shift your balance, leaning to make the turn (and thus cutting the edges of your skis into the snow), the front of each ski bites into the snow more than the back, grips the snow and your weight then pushes the backs of the skis around the front — and magically, you are turning. (At a higher level of skiing skill, this hour-glass shape of the ski is used differently, to "carve" turns. But that's for experts, not beginners — remember we must use learning gradients!)

Now the trick to all this, when you are teaching skiers, is that when they know this piece of theory they can *use* it. They now know the edges of their skis are their friends that help them make turns, and help hold them onto the mountain — not those nasty, monstrous things that keep catching the snow and tripping them up! And so, magically, they *use* those edges instead of *mis*using and running afoul of them.

There is also the reverse side of this coin.

Too Much Theory & an Absence of Mass or Physical Experience

You can also be bogged down with too much of the theory or significance of a subject and not have enough of the *action* or *mass* associated with the subject. In other words, you need the proper balance of these things that comprise the subject you are studying: the *theory* and *action* properly balanced, or the proper balance of the subject's *mass* and *significance*. In this circumstance mass and action equate, as also do theory and significance equate with each other.

An example: Very good big dictionaries don't just give you lots of words (theory and significance) on a physical object or thing they are defining; they will often give you a pictorial representation (its mass). Indeed, in this context a picture *is* worth a thousand words. You can suffer greatly when being made to study only the theory and significances of a subject in the absence of its mass or the doing of its actions! You can get to feeling quite ill (as described below).

If you happen to have a big dictionary that simply defines things without giving you pictures, you'll have a tough time and begin to experience the symptoms associated with studying without properly balancing the theory with its associated mass or action — and of course, you really won't get a happy comprehension and full knowingness of what this thing is you have been "reading about." We have included a drill at the end of this chapter that will give you the chance to experience these phenomena.

How to Recognize When You Have an Imbalance of Theoretical Knowledge versus Practical Experience

Trying to learn in the presence of an absence of mass, that is, trying to learn something without having a physical representation of it or being able to do the action of it, will eventually cause the student to feel crushed and empty. The student will begin to feel squashed and bent out of shape, with a sort of weird discomfort and feeling of the pressure of a mass moving in and building up on him or her.

The student also experiences this pressure and squashedness when confronted with too much mass or action and insufficient of the theory of the how and why. Though when this happens in real life, this particular symptom can be masked by acute unease or real fear of the circumstances that the overwhelming mass or action presents. I well remember this when I once got onto a very difficult ski run while learning. It also happened to me as a boy learning to surf the big Pacific rollers, and again while learning to ride a horse. It was a case of too much mass, too much action, all of which was unbalanced due to insufficient "know-how."

Solving Imbalances

There are various ways one can remedy these imbalances. In the case of an absence of mass, getting the real object or engaging in the actual action is the best. You can also use diagrams, photos, pictures, model the item or concept in clay, or have a collection of odds and ends that can be made to represent the various parts and actions of the thing being studied, and use them in a demonstration of the concept. In the case of absence of theory or significance, finding a good coach or "how-to manual," or consulting theoretical texts and reference books does the job.

Here is a drill that will let you experience these phenomena.

DRILL SIX
RECOGNIZING AN IMBALANCE BETWEEN
ACTION & THEORY OR MASS & SIGNIFICANCE

Purpose: To give the student a subjective reality of what happens when they are studying, trying to learn, or dealing with anything in life in the presence of an imbalance of action & theory or mass & significance.

This drill has two parts. The first part will subject you to too much theory or significance which you will resolve by getting the mass to balance it. The second part will subject you to too much mass in the form of an unexplained diagram which you will resolve by obtaining the balancing significance and theory explanation.

Position: Student and coach seated together or opposite each other.

PART ONE

Directions: **Step 1.**

Select one of the following definitions you are not familiar with (taken from *American Heritage Dictionary, Second College Edition*.) Read that definition.

Brace: (noun) crank-like handle with an adjustable aperture at one end for securing and turning a bit.

Awl: (noun) a pointed instrument for piercing small holes in leather, wood, etc.

Okapi: (noun) an African forest mammal, related to the giraffe, but smaller and with a much shorter neck.

These two crosses have similar descriptions:
Ansate Cross — A cross like a T with a loop at the top,
Celtic Cross — An upright cross superimposed on a circle.

Step 2.

Now draw a picture of your understanding of this definition of the chosen word, or in the case of the two crosses above, draw your understanding of the difference between them. If you are stalled, unable to easily do so or otherwise confused or feeling fuzzy, notice how you feel, acknowledge it and go to Appendix 2 or a good big dictionary for a copy of a picture of the object in the definition.

Notice how you feel after you have seen the picture of the object and understand it more fully. Also notice how close or different your understanding of the object and your drawing of it was to the truth. Notice how getting some "mass" by way of the picture helped.

Step 3.

Ask Student: **Did anything trigger or come to mind while doing this drill?**

If so, say: **Tell me about it.** Acknowledge the answer with "OK" or "Thank you." Do not make any further comment, only acknowledge.

PART TWO

Directions: Part Two **Step 1.**

According to the dictionary definition, the three objects below are the same thing. They have the same name and definition. Do you know what they are? Do you know what they show? Do you know what the significance or meaning of them is?

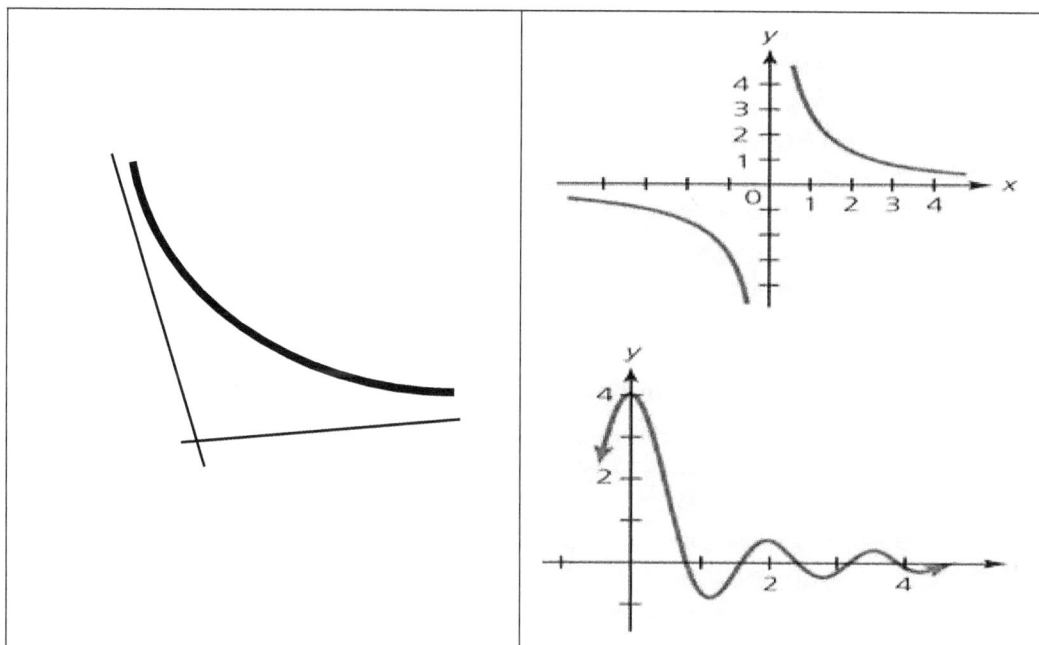

Step 2.

Try to explain the answers to those questions to your study partner. If you are stalled, unable to easily do so or otherwise confused or feeling fuzzy, notice how you feel, acknowledge it and go to Appendix 3 for the definition, explanation, significance and meaning of these objects.

Notice how you feel when you have balanced the mass of the objects with the significance and meaning of them.

Step 3.

Ask Student: **Did anything trigger or come to mind while doing this drill?**

If so, say: **Tell me about it.** Acknowledge the answer with "OK" or "Thank you." Do not make any further comment, only acknowledge.

Write up any wins, insights or cognitions.

CHAPTER EIGHT

LEARNING BARRIER SIX

LACK OF APPRECIATION

Appreciation is actually a big subject, and important in life and in learning. Many folk study, but fail to appreciate the worth, significance, and importance of what has been studied, and thus fail to recognize the value of, or apply correctly, what they have been exposed to.

Appreciate v. t. 1. to recognize the quality, significance, or magnitude of: *appreciated their freedom*. 2. to be fully aware of or sensitive to; realize: *I appreciate your problems*. 3. to be thankful or show gratitude for: *I really appreciate your help*. 4. to admire greatly; value. 5. to raise in value or price, especially over time. *v. i.* to increase in value or price, especially over time.

Synonyms: appreciate, value, prize, esteem, treasure, cherish.

These verbs mean to have a favorable opinion of someone or something.

Appreciate applies especially when high regard is based on critical assessment, comparison, and judgment: "As students so far from home, we have learned to appreciate those of life's pleasures that are not readily available in the People's Republic of China." (Sports Illustrated).

Value implies high regard for the importance or worth of the object: "In principle, the modern university values nothing more than the free exchange of ideas necessary for the pursuit of knowledge" (Eloise Salholz).

Prize often suggests pride of possession: "the nonchalance prized by teenagers" (Elaine Louie).

Esteem implies respect of a formal sort: "If he had never esteemed my opinion before, he would have thought highly of me then" (Jane Austen).

Treasure and *cherish* stress solicitous care for what is considered precious and often suggest affectionate regard: "We treasure our freedom". "They seek out the Salish Indian woman for the wisdom of her 86 years, and to learn the traditions she cherishes" (Tamara Jones).

Appreciation: noun 1. recognition of the quality, value, significance, or magnitude of people and things. 2. a judgment or opinion, especially a favorable one. 3. an expression of gratitude. 4. awareness or delicate perception, especially of aesthetic qualities or values. 5. a rise in value or price, especially over time.

Thus we see failure to appreciate the parts of what is being studied and learned, their significance, relative importance, applicability, use or value, will lead to a failure to fully comprehend the subject studied and failure to apply it to the optimum.

Value is Determined by Comparison

Part of the act of appreciating what is being learned is to be able to compare that to something of comparable magnitude. The comparable magnitude chosen can be either another truth, experience, the environment in which it applies, or the end result one wishes to obtain by its application.

Thus we see that a failure to properly and fully appreciate what has been learned can lead to a misalignment of what has been learned, a failure to properly use and apply what has been learned, the devaluing of what has been learned, the allowing of it to drop into non-use and then its being lost to use. It's part of the "use it or lose it" syndrome. (And we've all got instances of learned skills that we've allowed to fall into non-use and then lost that knowledge or ability.)

Drill Seven in the *Workbook of Exercises* in the Appendix will give you a subjective reality on the importance of appreciation as a part of learning. You may do it now, or when you read this manual the second time.

CHAPTER NINE

LEARNING BARRIER SEVEN

FAILURE TO RECOGNIZE OR ASSIGN CORRECT AND RELATIVE ORDERS OF IMPORTANCE

Orders of Importance: Failure to assign or recognize correct and relative orders of importance among the data and things being learned, results in incompetence and error of application. This is due to all things equaling all things, not knowing which to do first, which to align against which, or what the real objective of any action is.

On any subject there are some things that are vital for you to know and be able to do. Other things are merely useful; others are merely interesting. In the absence of knowing the correct and relative order of importance of things, you don't know what you **must** do versus what it is *merely good to do if you can.*

Absence of Importance

Modern American education fails in this. They don't assign the items of the subjects they are teaching their correct relative importance; the items are *all* presented as important, equally important, or otherwise the system stresses irrelevancies as grossly over important. I'm sure you've sat an exam that tested you on the irrelevant, while not testing you on what, to you, was so obviously important that you were sure you'd get a test on it.

Putting Order into What is Being Learned or Taught

Being able to assign relative and correct orders of importance to the various data of a subject actually puts *order* (as in orderliness and tidiness) into the subject. Things can then be classified properly. Certain data are primary to other data and give them meaning and relevance; other data merely add to, clarify or expand the prime datum or data.

Let's look at some examples of this.

What would you say are the orders of importance of items to be learned in the subject of reading and writing in any language? This is our list:

1. Recognition that language is a system of symbols and sounds that represent concepts and/or real things such that they can be communicated and related with. (A spoken word is simply a sound symbol representing a concept or condition of actuality.)

2. Understanding what those sounds (words) represent. (That is, what does each word mean; what are their definitions — what is the concept or thing conveyed when they are used.)

3. These spoken words have a system of symbols called the alphabet that represents the sounds in the words.

4. Knowing what those written symbols are, and what sounds each represent.

5. Knowing how these written symbols are combined to form the sounds of the spoken word.

6. Knowing that punctuation is used to express intonation, intent, the introduction of added relative thought or explanation, clarification and the ending of each complete thought or communication.

7. Knowing that grammar names and defines the functions of the parts of a communication, and conveys tense, possession, number, direct or indirect effect, etc.

This, also, is probably the sequence in which the subject should be taught.

In mathematics, our list would go something like this:

1. Mathematics is a system of measurement and calculation in dealing with quantities, magnitude and form and their relationship and attributes.

2. Math has its own system of symbols to represent these values and the functions used to compute values and relationships.

3. Knowing what the written symbols are that represent quantity and function.

4. Understanding what each function does, and how to perform each of them.

5. Mathematics has its own form of grammar and expression of terms.

6. Understanding this math grammar and use of terms.

In chemistry, the order of importance of data may go like this:

1. The underlying principles of why and how chemical elements combine or separate.

2. The periodic chart of elements and the alignment of elements therein.

These are the principles upon which the science of chemistry is now built, but these are not the sequence of items in which the subject would be taught.

Enabling Control of the Knowledge of a Subject

You will notice that we have highlighted the important points throughout this book. Otherwise, the reader might slip into the usual societal habit of seeing all points as equal and not really learning what it is they set out to learn. Without this the student would not have proper control of the subject and what is being learned.

For example, the opening words of Chapter 1 stated the orders of importance of truths needed to be known relative to this subject of education, teaching and learning:

1. The ability to learn is a faculty we all have. Young children do it naturally.

2. When there is difficulty in learning, there is something getting in the way.

3. We then delineated the Seven Barriers to Comprehension that get in the way and impede the natural ability to learn.

4. We then provided answers as to how to prevent these barriers from interfering with the learning process.

Knowing these four points, and knowing them in this sequence is vitally important for any parent or teacher. Why? If these truths are not known, parents, teachers and their advisors can come to some catastrophically wrong answers in the handling of our children. That may shock you, but we invite you to consider the statistics of how many children nowadays are being labeled "learning disabled," "dull," "impaired," "troubled" or such and then are wrongly handled.

This did not happen fifty-sixty years ago. When I went to school, everyone was literate.

Now, there are some greater truths in the subject of human ability than are expressed here, but they are for later on up the road — remember our truth about gradients; we practice it. The ability to learn is a key basic ability, but one of many we human beings are blessed with.

Drill Eight in the *Workbook of Exercises* in the Appendix has Parts Two and Three to be done as appropriate, or on your second reading of this manual. Part One of Drill Eight follows, and should be done now.

ADDENDUM

The nine chapters of this manual you have just read were written with the data presented in the sequence you will actually encounter the phenomena, not in order of biggest or most important truth. Once again, you see the application of correct gradient; all items needed to be known at each stage of the way are made available, nothing skipped or gotten out of order. That's an important datum, but perhaps the most important datum in this section is the datum about correct definitions. If you are not honest and thorough on that, you will *always* fail. It's that important. We'll leave you to ponder on the value of the rest of what you have just read here.

****

DRILL EIGHT

PART ONE
ASSIGNING CORRECT & RELATIVE ORDERS OF IMPORTANCE

Purpose of the Exercise: To give the student a subjective reality of how assigning correct relative orders of importance puts order into an otherwise confused scenario of learning and ensures that the most important items are learned or performed, and that this is also true in other activities in life.

Step 1.

   Coach has the student do the following actions:

   a) Look at your daily life. Note the large number of actions you perform (Example: staying alive, sleep, breath, eat, bathe, travel, work, study, play, do housework, cook, etc.).

   b) Write a list of ten to twelve (or more) daily actions you perform.

   c) Now number or re-arrange them in correct order of importance on the basis of:

     imperative and most vital

     vital

     important

     useful

     interesting or

     entertainment only.

   d) Evaluate how you have ordered these items. Do you notice the imperative, most vital action is supported by all the other actions? Do you notice the imperative, most vital action is the reason for all the other actions?

Step 2.

   Ask Student: **Did anything trigger or come to mind while doing this drill?**

   If so, say: **Tell me about it.** Acknowledge the answer with "OK" or "Thank you." Do not make any further comment, only acknowledge.

Write up any wins, insights or cognitions.

CHAPTER TEN

MASTERING THE LEARNING PROCESS

HOW LEARNING MASTERS OPERATE

Studying is the action and process one carries out to learn something.

Learning is the successful outcome of a correctly applied study process or procedure, which results in the intended accomplishment of full comprehension of that which one wants to understand, along with being able to successfully apply the materials and concepts learned.

Those are important and rather precise definitions of study and learning. And it is worth having a good look at them to fully digest all of their parts. For some folks, they may actually need to be sure they truly comprehend the meanings of the key words contained in them, and to use a dictionary where necessary.

Masters of the learning process do not impede themselves, or trip up, by ever leaving unhandled any barriers to comprehension they encounter or create. They do not *ever* leave unhandled any non-comprehensions or barriers to comprehension . . . *ever*.

Masters of the teaching process do not inflict on their students any barriers to comprehension; nor do they fail to perceive and fully resolve any manifestations of the presence of comprehension barriers that the student collides with or creates.

How is mastery in each of these two aspects of the educational process achieved? By practice of the drills in this manual, and by *constant* practice and application of the knowledge you gain from using what you are reading in this manual.

Thus another vitally important aspect of attaining mastery in learning is that of practice, practice, practice.

Have you noticed that your greatest athletes practice, practice, practice? They spend hours upon hours at practice in the pursuit of perfecting their skills.

This is the mark of a *master*! Masters practice, practice, practice till they know they have mastered the skill, ability or knowledge they seek.

The current educational system in our schools and universities does not afford its students the opportunity to practice what is being learned in a manner sufficient to attain mastery. Nor does the system require students take anything to mastery. Indeed, the system is rigged such that only superficial, light contact is made across the spectrum of what is presented to students. And the result is that students end up with a deep-down awareness that they really don't know the materials as they ought to, and nothing is taken to mastery.

This has catastrophic consequences in life. As an example: I recently saw a statistic that stated nearly one-fifth of all medical diagnoses in America are erroneous! (See endnote2) One is constantly being reminded in the media of engineering works that have failed because of faulty design or construction.

A good example of practicing to a level of mastery is that applied by the American airline industry. We are all grateful that our pilots are made do so!

THE IMPORTANCE OF LEARNING AND ITS EFFECT ON A SUCCESSFUL LIFE.

It has been said that learning is a life-long process. That is true; but it is not a whole truth.

It misses the most important point.

What is most important about learning and life is that without continuous learning you will fail to live up to your full potential in virtually all the endeavors you engage in. Or to put it in positive terms, being able to continuously learn in all circumstances is essential to your success in life.

Successful Living Involves Constant Learning

There is virtually no activity you engage in that does not involve an ongoing learning action, or the use of your ability to learn and comprehend.

Life is a constantly changing scenario. Every activity one is engaged in presents new situations, information or aspects of relationship. And these have to be, *must be*, comprehended.

No successful relationship, whether marriage, business, sporting or friendship, can be had unless one can learn and then comprehend:

a) what the other person(s) needs or wants,

b) how to deliver that need or want,

c) what the other person does not want and,

d) how to not abuse the other person with, or give them, what they don't want.

Relationships fail because of the lack of comprehension. Businesses fail because of lack of comprehension and the inability to learn. Sports contests and matches are lost because of failure to learn while engaged in the game or through lack of comprehension. Friendships end because of failure to learn or comprehend what the other person is up to, or needs and wants.

Even one's relationships in or with the physical universe: fishing, hunting, sailing, skiing, any hobby, balancing a check-book, or even finding your way around the New York City Subway System requires the ability to learn and comprehend.

Without the ability to learn being successfully practiced, you will fail in every endeavor in life. The ability to learn — the ability to perceive and comprehend what is extant and going on around one is essential to one's survival as well as to one's success in every endeavor.

And this is an ongoing, continuous function.

If one does not learn; if one allows oneself to be thwarted by the presence of the *barriers to comprehension*, or violations of *the twelve vital fundamentals of life processes*, one will fail in life and all its endeavors.

Non-Comprehensions Accumulate & Destroy Liveliness

If you inspect this in your own experience, you will find that non-comprehension is a cumulative thing. Non-comprehensions accumulate and compound on you. They are very much the essence of the "aging process".

The more non-comprehensions one accumulates, the less interest one begins to have in life and its adventures. The more set in one's ways, the more in the rut, one becomes. And as we saw in Chapter Five, non-comprehension immobilizes one and prevents the ability to act. You end up dulled and boxed in, all because of non-comprehension.

And thus one's "liveliness" is lost. And it all stems from not knowing how to learn, the inability to learn, or the failure to practice the correct learning processes in a masterly manner.

Don't do that to yourself. Learn and apply what is in this manual.

APPENDIX

And

ADDENDUM

The beginning of wisdom is the definition of terms.

Socrates (470 - 399 BC)

CLEAN SLATE HANDLING LEARNING DRILL

Definitions:

YOU: The Spiritual Being; the life-force; the energizer.

TERM: *n.* 1. A word having a precise meaning. 2. Any word or phrase used in a definite or precise sense. Synonyms: word, vocable, phrase, locution, expression

WORD: *n.* 1. A sound or a combination of sounds, or its representation in writing or printing, that symbolizes and communicates a meaning. 2. Something that is said; an utterance, remark, or comment.

VOCABLE: *n.* A word considered only as a sequence of sounds or letters rather than as a unit of meaning.

PHRASE: *n.* 1. Any sequence of words intended to have meaning. 2. A word or group of words read or spoken as a unit and separated by pauses or other junctures.

LOCUTION: *n.* A particular word, phrase, or expression considered from the point of view of style.

EXPRESSION: *n.* 1. The act of expressing, conveying or representing in words, art, music, or movement; manifestation. 2. That which symbolizes something; a symbol; a sign, a token.

PRECEPT: *n.* 1. A prescribed rule of conduct or action; instruction or direction. 2. Instruction or direction regarding a given course of action, especially a maxim in morals. The basis and source of a belief system.

BELIEF SYSTEM: A belief system is the set of a person's interrelated ideas, principles, precepts, rules, or laws that governs their acceptance or conviction in the actuality of something they perceive. It is the person's mindset. Belief systems are created by the person's knowledge and experiences.

Important note: At all times, the student should define any terms that are not fully comprehended by looking them up in the dictionary or glossary before going on.

0.   *One person reads a paragraph of the material being studied, or describes the area or subject (breaking it down into its parts) to be cleaned. The other person then addresses the term, paragraph, area, or subject part by asking:*

1.   **What is your comprehension of this?**

        Have the person look inward at their concepts, visions, or models for their answer and tell you what they experience. If they present a clean, precise comprehension with certainty, go to Step 2. If they encounter confusion, pain, a gap of blackness, or stupidity, have them go to a dictionary and get the terms defined. When they have a clean vision, concept, or comprehension, acknowledge them and ask:

2. **Does that trigger or remind you of anything?**

    Have the person look inward for the answer.

    Tell me your perceptions about that. .

    Acknowledge their answer.

3. **What precepts, beliefs or thoughts do you have about or from <u>(thing being addressed from step 0)</u>?**

    Get the person to look inward for the answer and to tell you the precept, belief or thought. By asking the person to look inward, you are directing their attention to their comprehension, visions, concepts, or mind. Acknowledge their answer.

    k. **Connected to <u>(named precept/belief/thought)</u>, where is it?**

    Acknowledge their answer.

    l. **Connected to <u>(named precept/belief/thought)</u>, what is its size?**

    Acknowledge their answer.

    m. **Connected to <u>(named precept/belief/thought)</u>, what is its form or shape?**

    Acknowledge their answer.

    n. **Connected to <u>(named precept/belief/thought)</u>, what is its color?**

    Acknowledge their answer.

    o. **Connected to <u>(named precept/belief/thought)</u>, what is its weight?**

    Acknowledge their answer.

    p. **Connected to <u>(named precept/belief/thought)</u>, what is its duration?**

    Acknowledge their answer.

    q. **Connected to <u>(named precept/belief/thought)</u>, what are its mood levels?**

    Acknowledge their answer.

    r. **Connected to <u>(named precept/belief/thought)</u>, what are its limitations?**

    Acknowledge their answer.

    s. **Connected to <u>(named precept/belief/thought)</u>, what must not be experienced?**

    Acknowledge their answer.

    t. **Connected to <u>(named precept/belief/thought)</u>, what must be experienced?**

    Acknowledge their answer.

4. **Does <u>(named precept/belief/thought)</u> create an image or vision?** *If "Yes," say:*

    Tell me about it.

5. **How does <u>(named precept/belief/thought)</u> manifest in your presence-time?**

6a. **What have been or could be the consequences of having that precept/belief/thought?**

Acknowledge their answer.

6b.   **Have there been or could there be any other consequences?**

Acknowledge their answer.

Repeat Step 6b until all consequences have been viewed.

7.   **Do you have any other precepts, beliefs or thoughts about or from <u>(thing being addressed from step 0)</u>?**

Repeat questions 4 to 7 until all precepts on the thing being addressed have been viewed. Then have the person reread the paragraph of the material being studied, or describe the area or subject (breaking it down into its parts) being cleaned, and ask:

8.   **Connected to <u>(thing being addressed from step 0)</u>, do you have any misdefined   terms?**

Get the terms and fully define them in the dictionary. Repeat #8 until all misdefined terms have been found and fully comprehended, then ask:

9.   **What would be the consequences of having the ability to <u>(whatever the ability would be for thing being addressed from step 0)</u>?**

Acknowledge their answer.

10.   **What dream or goal does comprehending <u>(thing being addressed from step 0)</u> contribute to or support?**

Have them tell you about it and acknowledge their answer.

11.   **What problem does comprehending <u>(thing being addressed from step 0)</u> solve?**

Have them tell you about it and acknowledge their answer.

12.   **What vision does comprehending <u>(thing being addressed from step 0)</u> create or reinforce?**

Have them tell you about it and acknowledge their answer.

15 May 1987   ALAN C. WALTER
Revised 13 April 2005
By Roger E. Boswarva

APPENDIX TWO
Pictures for Drill Six Part One

awl

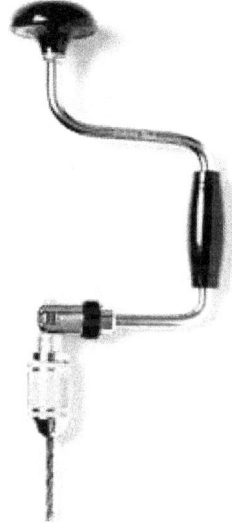

Brace
(with drill-bit secured ready to use)

okapi

Ansate Cross

Celtic Cross

APPENDIX THREE
Pictures for Drill Six Part Two

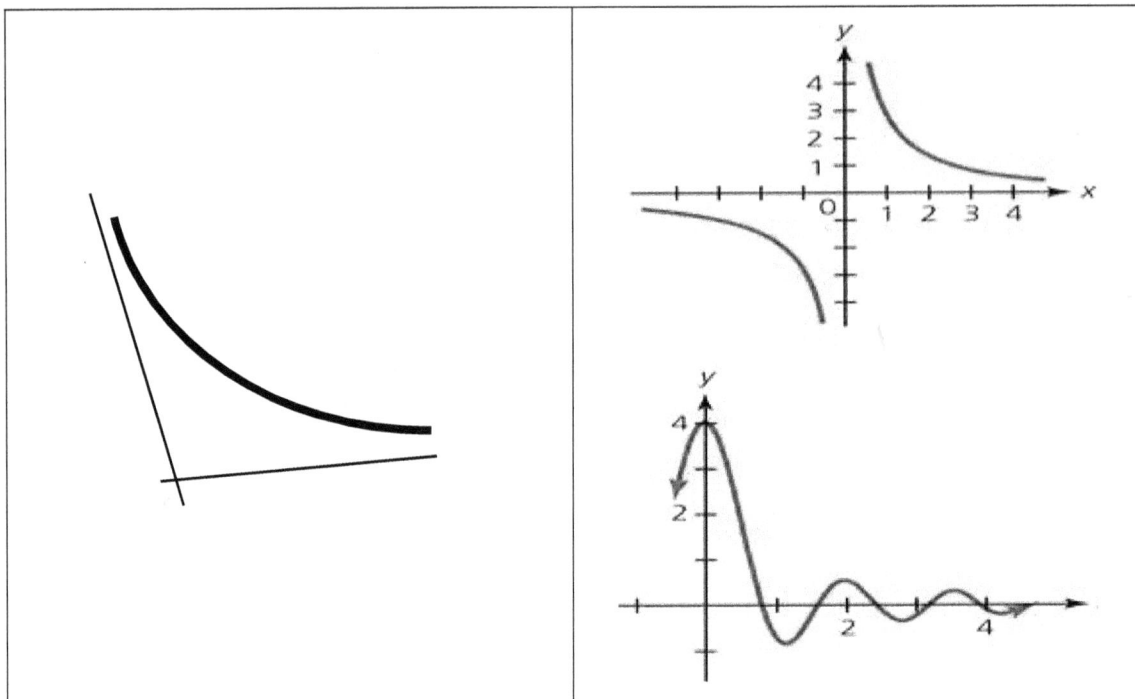

These are **asymptotes.** Various dictionaries define *asymptote* differently though give the same meaning.

Webster's New World Dictionary, from the World Publishing Company states:
Asymptote: in mathematics, a straight line always approaching but never meeting a curve; tangent at infinity.

The American Heritage Dictionary states:
Asymptote: (noun) Math. A line considered a limit to a curve in the sense that the perpendicular distance from a moving point on the curve to the line approaches zero as the point moves an infinite distance from the origin.

Webster's New Collegiate Dictionary, from G. & C. Merriam Company states:
Asymptote: n. a straight line associated with a curve such that as a point moves along an infinite branch of the curve the distance from the point to the line approaches zero and the slope of the curve at the point approaches the slope of the line.

Now you know why it is a good idea to have several dictionaries for getting definitions. Some are clear and concise and others are rather rambling and unclear. Note that the "Merriam Webster" does not state that this is a term which applies in mathematics as the other dictionaries do. One on-line web dictionary actually gives an incorrect definition, stating an asymptote is a curve.

Workbook of Exercises

For

Barriers to Comprehension

DRILL ONE

Understanding the Purpose of the Subject & Your Intention for Studying It.

Purpose of the Exercise: To give the student a subjective reality of how studying a subject without knowing the purpose or use of the subject, and having a worthwhile intention for studying it, can cause the student to not learn the subject fully or misuse the knowledge gained.

This drill can be done with a study partner who acts as coach, or done "solo" by oneself.

Part One
Using a good dictionary write down the complete definition of the following words:

Purpose: _____
_____
_____
_____

Intention: _____
_____
_____
_____

Write down your understanding of:

"Purpose of the Subject": _____
_____
_____
_____

"Intention for Studying It":
_____
_____
_____
_____

Part Two

Write down what the purpose is for each subject listed below, and what your intention is for studying it.

Reading

Purpose: _____

_____

_____

_____

Intention: _____

_____

_____

_____

Writing & Composition

Purpose: _____

_____

_____

_____

Intention: _____

_____

_____

_____

Math

Purpose: _____

_____

_____

_____

Intention: _____

_____

_____

_____

Science

Purpose: _____

_____

_____
_____

Intention: _____
_____
_____
_____

Physical Education
Purpose: _____
_____
_____
_____

Intention: _____
_____
_____
_____

Art
Purpose: _____
_____
_____
_____

Intention: _____
_____
_____
_____

Music
Purpose: _____
_____
_____
_____

Intention: _____
_____
_____
_____

(Insert Your Own Subject)
Purpose: _____

_____
_____
_____

Intention: _____

_____
_____
_____

(Insert Your Own Subject)
Purpose: _____

_____
_____
_____

Intention: _____

_____
_____
_____

(Insert Your Own Subject)
Purpose: _____

_____
_____
_____

Intention: _____

_____
_____
_____

(Insert Your Own Subject)
Purpose: _____

_____
_____
_____

Intention: _____

_____

_____

_____

(Insert Your Own Subject)
Purpose: _____

_____

_____

_____

Intention: _____

_____

_____

_____

DRILL ONE

PART THREE

1.   Check yourself: Are there any subject(s) you were made to study for which you saw no purpose. If so, write it/them down.

2.   Acknowledge that at that time you saw no use or purpose for the subject, and that you may have been disinclined to pay adequate attention.

3.   Can you conceive of any value or purpose for the subjects now? Write them down.

Write up any Wins, Insights or Cognitions.

It is extremely important that you properly recognize, acknowledge, validate, honor and appreciate any wins, insights or sudden AHA's! We call these cognitions. It is a word that is not in all dictionaries, but it means: "to become suddenly or extremely aware or cognizant of something". A big breakthrough in knowledge and/or ability to perform would such an event; and all such wins must be honored, appreciated so they can be fully empowered and continue to be under your knowing future control. There is an old saying: *"Use it or lose it"*.

See Appendix 6 for an explanation for the reason it is important to write-up one's wins and have them properly honored and appreciated.

Appendix 5 is a very important and useful process for fully validating, stabilizing and actualizing

DRILL TWO

Experiencing Precepts & False Notions of What is Correct or Should Be

Purpose of the Exercise: To give the student a subjective reality of how precepts and false notions of what should be, can get in the way of learning and/or the correct application of what was learned.

Position: Partners sit opposite each other close enough to have knees just about touching.

Part One

A. One partner will be the Coach/Sender and the other partner will be the Student receiving.
   a) The Student receiver will adopt the mood/attitude that "they already know" all about what the Coach will read.
   b) The Coach reads a definition from the dictionary or a passage from a book.
   c) The Coach than asks the Student what he or she received and understood. Acknowledge the answer, with "OK," or "Thank you". Do not make any further comment, only acknowledge.
   d) The Coach then asks the Student to "Describe what you perceived happen while I was reading this material to you." The Coach acknowledges the answer, and then asks:
   e) **"Did anything trigger or come to mind while doing this drill?"**
   f) If so, say: **"Tell me about it."** Acknowledge the answer.
   g) The Coach and Student reverse roles. The Student receiver now asks of the Coach sender to **"Describe what you perceived happen while you were reading to me."** The Student acknowledges the answer, and then asks:
   h) **"Did anything trigger or come to mind while doing this drill?"**
   i) If so, say: **"Tell me about it."** Acknowledge the answer with "OK" or "Thank you". Do not make any further comment, only acknowledge.

B. The Coach Sender will again read from the dictionary or a book.
   a) This time the Student receiver will adopt the mood/attitude of "I want to know all about it" while the Coach reads.
   b) The Coach reads a definition from the dictionary or a passage from a book.
   c) The Coach then asks the Student what he or she received and understood. Acknowledge the answer.
   d) The Coach then asks the Student to **"Describe what you perceived happen while you were receiving what I read."** The Coach acknowledges the answer, and then asks:

e) **"Did anything trigger or come to mind while doing this drill?"**

f) If so, say: **"Tell me about it."** Acknowledge the answer with "OK" or "Thank you". Do not make any further comment, only acknowledge.

g) The Coach and Student now reverse roles. The Student receiver then asks of the Coach sender to **"Describe what you perceived happen while you were reading to me."** The Student acknowledges the answer, and then asks:

h) **"Did anything trigger or come to mind while doing this drill?"**

i) If so, say: **"Tell me about it."** Acknowledge the answer with "OK" or "Thank you". Do not make any further comment, only acknowledge.

Write up any Wins, Cognitions or Insights.

Part Two

Do Clean Slate Handling Learning Drill on the following:

Study
Learning
The concept/action of: "Studying to Learn"

See Appendix 1 for the Clean Slate Learning Drill

DRILL THREE
RECOGNIZING NON-COMPREHENSIONS

Purpose: To give the student a subjective reality of the fact that in the presence of incompletely defined, non-defined or misunderstood words, terms and symbols a person goes mentally blank, immobile, and is unable to perform; and if forced to act will likely do so in error.

Position Student and coach seated together or opposite each other with a good big dictionary

Directions   **Step One:**

Coach commands the student to do one of the following actions (each are to do different phrases):

a) "**Demonstrate to me the concept 'when crepuscule came the children ran inside'.**"

b) "**Demonstrate to me the concept 'when crepitating began the children became afraid'.**"

c) "**Demonstrate to me the concept 'when the children found the creodont they were rewarded'.**"

If the student at all pauses, stalls, or is otherwise non-performing or gone mentally blank, the coach is to say: "**I notice you are not performing, what is the word you don't have a clear definition for?**" Coach is to then have student consult the dictionary and obtain a full comprehension of the word(s). Don't be surprised at which words the student doesn't clearly understand and has to look up. Then the coach again commands the student to perform the incomplete demonstration. (Anything in the environment may be used in the demonstration including a collection of small items such as paperclips, pencils, rubber-bands, matches, etc. These items can be made represent the parts or people and actions in the demonstration)

Step Two:

Ask Student: "**Did anything trigger or come to mind while doing this drill?**"

If so, say: "**Tell me about it.**" Acknowledge the answer with "OK" or "Thank you". Do not make any further comment, only acknowledge.

******

DRILL FOUR
CLARIFYING MISUNDERSTOOD & ABSENT DEFINITIONS

Purpose of the Exercise: To give the student a subjective reality of how freeing it is to clarify incompletely understood or misunderstood words or terms.

Part One
Write down your current understanding of:

Prefix: _____
_____
_____
_____

Mis: _____
_____
_____
_____

Non: _____
_____
_____
_____

Look up these words in a good dictionary and write down their definitions.

Prefix: _____
_____
_____
_____

Mis: _____
_____
_____
_____

Non: _____
_____
_____
_____

How does your definition compare to or differ from the dictionary definition?

If the definitions were quite different, can you spot when, where and from whom you received your definition? Did you invent your own definition in the place of (absence of) the correct definition?

Remove any incorrect definition from your mind and replace it with the correct dictionary definition (if this has not already happened).

Write up any Wins, Insights or Cognitions.

Part Two
    a) Doing this drill may have triggered or called to mind times you went past an incompletely understood, non-understood or misunderstood word or symbol.
    b) If so, write down each such word or symbol.
    c) Using a good dictionary, define each such word or symbol.
    d) When you have the opportunity, re-read the material where you earlier went past these non-understood words or symbols and recover the knowledge.
    e) While it may take some time, it is a very fruitful exercise to address the subjects that are important to you to erase all non-comprehensions caused by non-defined, incompletely defined or misunderstood words, terms or symbols. You will recover a vast amount of clarity and intelligence.

Write up any Wins, Insights or Cognitions.

DRILL FIVE
RECOGNIZING BY-PASSED GRADIENTS

Purpose: To give the student a subjective reality of what happens when a study or learning gradient is missed.

Position Student and coach seated together or opposite each other with a pad of paper and pen, pencil or even a calculator.

Directions   **Step One:**
Coach commands the student to do the following action:
"Perform the following sequence of calculations in your mind: 2 times 2 are 4, 2 times 4 are 8, 2 times 8 are 16 and continue multiplying the product of each multiplication again by two as far as you can go mentally until you lose control of the calculation."

Coach waits until the student reaches his or her point of confusion or lost control of ability to continue mentally calculating. When the student indicates he or she has reached the point of lost control, acknowledge, and say the following: **"Now take the pen and paper and, in writing, repeat the last two calculations you had control of and continue the sequence of calculations two levels past where you just stopped."**

When the student has done so, ask: **"What did you notice happen?"**

Acknowledge his or her answer.

Step Two:
Ask Student: **"Did anything trigger or come to mind while doing this drill?"**
If so, say: **"Tell me about it."** Acknowledge the answer with "OK" or "Thank you". Do not make any further comment, only acknowledge.

Note this drill also employs the principle of introducing a mass or physical action to balance the thought and significance process (see "Learning Barrier Five" in chapter seven).

Write up any wins, insights or cognitions.

DRILL FIVE
PART TWO
HANDLING BY-PASSED GRADIENTS

Purpose: 1) To handle any by-passed gradients that may have been triggered or called to mind while studying the forgoing chapter or doing Part One of this drill. 2) To give the student a subjective reality of what happens when a missed study or learning gradient is corrected.

Position: Coach and student seated comfortably together or opposite each other.

Directions
   Step 1. Coach asks the student: "While reading this chapter or doing the drill, did any past study confusion, inability to perform or by-passed gradient get triggered or come to view?" If so:
   a) Ask student, "when was that earlier confusion, inability to perform or by-passed gradient?" Acknowledge answer.
   b) "Where did it occur? Acknowledge answer.
   c) "What was the subject you were studying?" Acknowledge answer.
   d) Ask the student to, "*Go earlier in the study of that subject to when you were doing well.*" Have the student let you know when they are there.
   e) Have the student re-check or demonstrate competence of that earlier in the study course winning point. Acknowledge it when done.
   f) Now trace forward to the next step or action of study in that past course and help the student master it. Apply any and all of the actions noted in this manual, as needed, to help the student master this earlier missed gradient. It is possible the missed gradient was never even presented to the student for study or practice; discovering this might have to be part of the debugging process.
   Going past a non-defined word, or having a misunderstood word, are examples of other barriers to comprehension that could be the cause of a by-passing of a gradient. It is to be noted that the step the student is stuck on or having difficulty with is *not* the by-passed gradient. The by-passed gradient is earlier at a lower learning or study level and it is that is causing the student to later have difficulty at the higher, later level.
   g) Have the student restudy and learn to a level of competence the later material(s) or action(s) that followed the by-passed gradient: that is, the material or actions where difficulty manifested due to the earlier by-passed gradient.

Step 2:

Ask Student: **"Did anything trigger or come to mind while doing this drill?"**

If so, say: **"Tell me about it."** Acknowledge the answer with "OK" or "Thank you". Do not make any further comment, only acknowledge.

Write up any Wins, Cognitions or Insights.

DRILL SIX
RECOGNIZING AN IMBALANCE BETWEEN
ACTION & THEORY OR MASS & SIGNIFICANCE

Purpose: To give the student a subjective reality of what happens when they are studying, trying to learn, or dealing with anything in life in the presence of an imbalance of action & theory or mass & significance.

This drill has two parts. The first part will subject you to too much theory or significance which you will resolve by getting the mass to balance it. The second part will subject you to too much mass in the form of an unexplained diagram which you will resolve by obtaining the balancing significance and theory explanation.

Position Student and coach seated together or opposite each other.

Directions Part One **Step One:**

Select one of the following definitions you are not familiar with (taken from American Heritage Dictionary, Second College Edition.) Read that definition.

Brace: (noun) crank-like handle with an adjustable aperture at one end for securing and turning a bit.

Awl: (noun) a pointed instrument for piercing small holes in leather, wood, etc.

Okapi: (noun) An African forest mammal, related to the giraffe, but smaller and with a much shorter neck.

These two crosses have similar descriptions:
Ansate Cross — A *cross* like a T with a loop at the top,
Celtic Cross — An upright cross superimposed on a circle.

Step two:

Now draw a picture of your understanding of this definition of the chosen word or, in the case of the two crosses draw your understanding of the difference between them. If you are stalled, unable to easily do so or otherwise confused or feeling fuzzy, notice how you feel, acknowledge it, and go to appendix 2 or a good big dictionary for a copy of a picture of the object in the definition.
Notice how you feel after you have seen the picture of the object and understand it more fully. Also notice how close, or different, your

understanding of the object and your drawing of it was to the truth. Notice how getting some "mass" by way of the picture helped.

Step Three:

Ask Student: **"Did anything trigger or come to mind while doing this drill?"**

If so, say: **"Tell me about it."** Acknowledge the answer with "OK" or "Thank you". Do not make any further comment, only acknowledge.

PART TWO

Directions Part Two **Step One:**

According to the dictionary definition, the three objects below are the same thing. They have the same name and definition. Do you know what they are? Do you know what they show? Do you know what the significance or meaning of them is?

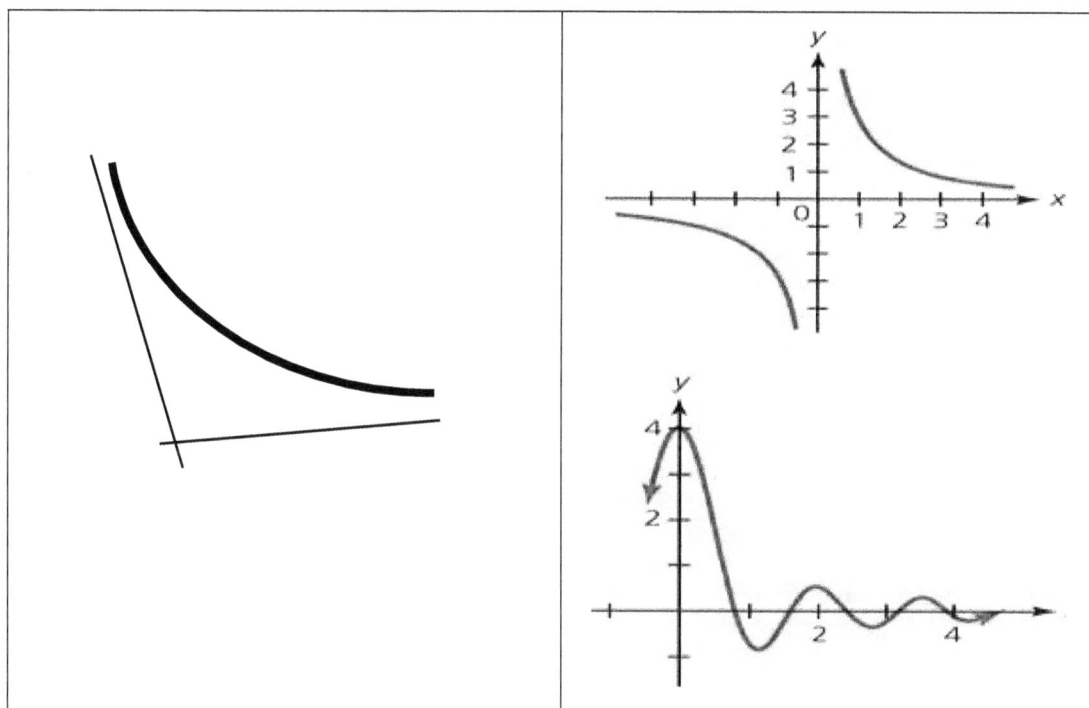

Step Two

Try to explain the answers to those questions to your study partner. If you are stalled, unable to easily do so or otherwise confused or feeling fuzzy, notice how you feel, acknowledge it, and go to appendix 3 for the definition, explanation, significance and meaning of these objects. Notice how you feel when you have balanced the mass of the objects with the significance and meaning of them.

Step Three:

Ask Student: **"Did anything trigger or come to mind while doing this drill?"**

If so, say: **"Tell me about it."** Acknowledge the answer with "OK" or "Thank you". Do not make any further comment, only acknowledge.

Write up any wins, insights or cognitions.

DRILL SEVEN
APPRECIATION

Purpose of the Exercise: To give the student a subjective reality of the importance of appreciation and how to appreciate, comparatively evaluate, and be able to come to a full recognition of the value, importance and significance of what has been learned.

a) Make a list of all the subjects and/or actions you have learned or can do well.

b) Take each subject or action and evaluate your level of competence from beginner to masterful. Use a scale of $1-10$.

c) Now list the component parts of each subject or action — all the parts needed to be learned and mastered to be able to perform the entire subject or action.

d) Now correctly recognize the value of what you have accomplished and give yourself appreciation and value for what you've achieved.

e) Notice how you feel about yourself and your abilities now.

f) Write up any Wins, Cognitions or Insights.

Example: Cooking
Component parts: learning terminology, storage & handling of raw ingredients, understanding flavors of various foods, flavors of spices and sauces, learning preparation, temperature control, cooking times for various ingredients, presentation of the meal. Use as many sheets as is needed for this exercise.

_____
_____
_____

_____
_____
_____

_____
_____
_____

_____
_____
_____

DRILL EIGHT

PART ONE
ASSIGNING CORRECT & RELATIVE ORDERS OF IMPORTANCE

Purpose of the Exercise: To give the student a subjective reality of how assigning correct relative orders of importance puts order into an otherwise confused scenario of learning, and ensures that the most important items are learned or performed; and that this is also true in other activities in life.

Step One:

    Coach has the student do the following actions:

    a) Look at your daily life. Note the large number of actions you perform (example: staying alive, sleep, breath, eat, bathe, travel, work, study, play, do housework, cook, etc.).

    b) Write a list of ten to twelve (or more) daily actions you perform.

    c) Now number or re-arrange them in correct order of importance on the basis of:

        imperative and most vital

        vital

        important

        useful

        interesting or

        entertainment only.

    d) Evaluate how you have ordered these items. Do you notice the imperative most vital action is supported by all the other actions? Do you notice the imperative most vital action is the reason for all the other actions?

Step Two:

    Ask Student: **"Did anything trigger or come to mind while doing this drill?"**

    If so, say: **"Tell me about it."** Acknowledge the answer with "OK" or "Thank you". Do not make any further comment, only acknowledge.

Write up any wins, insights or cognitions.

DRILL EIGHT

PART TWO

This is for more advanced students, not for younger children.

Purpose of the Exercise: To give the student a subjective reality on how the lesser important things depend on the vital and most important things.

Position: Coach has the student do the following:

a) Addressing the student's understanding of the subject of mathematics, the coach asks the following:

b) "What does knowing the multiplication tables enable you to do?" Acknowledge the answer. (This drill can also be done using the alphabet and its phonetics.)

c) "What other math actions are able to be done by use of the multiplication tables?" Acknowledge the answer. (Coach may coach with guidance. i.e. division, square roots, logarithms etc.)

d) "How important are the multiplication tables to the subject of mathematics?" Acknowledge the answer.

Write up any wins, insights or cognitions.

DRILL EIGHT

PART THREE

Purpose: To give the student a subjective reality on being able to discern distinctions as to whether items or things that are identical, similar, or different; and thus enable the student to differentiate and order them correctly as to importance.

Step One
Using a good dictionary look up the following words and write down their definitions:

Same: _____
_____
_____
_____

Similar: _____
_____
_____
_____

Different: _____
_____
_____
_____

Step Two
a.   Coach selects any two objects
b.   Ask student: "What is the same about these two objects?" Acknowledge answer.
c.   Ask: "What is similar about these two objects?" Acknowledge answer.
d.   Ask: "What is different about these two objects?" Acknowledge answer.
e.   Coach selects another pair of objects, and repeats the questions b. c. d. Continue this drill, selecting new objects each time, until the student has a win such as a big realization, or is certain they now can distinguish sameness (identicalness), similarities, and differences.

Step Three
Using a good dictionary, look up *Order* and write down as many definitions that would apply to *"Orders of Importance."*

_____
_____
_____

Using a good dictionary, look up *Importance* and *Important,* and write down the definitions.

_____
_____
_____
_____
_____
_____

Now write down your understanding of the concept of **Orders of Importance**.

_____
_____
_____
_____
_____
_____

How can you apply the principle of **Orders of Importance** to your life and what you do in life?

_____
_____
_____
_____
_____
_____
_____
_____
_____
_____
_____

Write up any Wins, Cognitions or Insights.

FUTURE ALIGNMENT PROCESS

To be done on all staff every day and on all clients who have had regained abilities, and after each successful completion of each major procedure.

"Tell me an ability you have regained."

1.   **"How could you implement the (<u>named ability</u>) to help another or others?**

     Repeat over and over to Cause Indicators.

2.   **"How could another or others implement the (<u>named ability</u>) to help you?**

     Repeat over and over to Cause Indicators.

3.   **"How could another or others implement the (<u>named ability</u>) to help others?**

     Repeat over and over to Cause Indicators.

4.   **"How could you implement the (<u>named ability</u>) to help yourself?**

     Repeat over and over to Cause Indicators.

Repeat 1 – 4 on each regained ability.

The product of this procedure is a person who can implement the abilities they have regained from training and processing to help create expanding futures for self and others.

ALAN C. WALTER

1 December 1995
Revised 6 December 1995

THE PURPOSE AND POWER OF WRITING SUCCESS STORIES

Definitions:

SUCCESS: *n*. The achievement of something desired, planned or attempted.

STORY: *n*. The narrating or relating of an event or series of events.

American Heritage Dictionary

It is vital you understand the power that writing success stories restores to you.

When you attain a win, regain an ability, or recover a state of being, the change first occurs in your own universe. If you do nothing further with it, that is where it stays, in your own universe.

When you tell another or others about the win, ability or state it can become part of their universe too. But, it is still limited as at best the new knowledge, ability or beingness can only be utilized between you and those you have told.

However, when you write a Success Story recounting the recovery of and describing the win, ability or state, you have entered the win, ability or state into the physical universe and it stays there.

The physical universe is the playing field where you operate and play the games of life. To utilize your newly attained knowledge, abilities and states you must bring them into the physical universe.

Writing Success Stories adds your regained awareness, knowledge, abilities, and states to your position in the physical universe, adding to your power, strength and ability to win at the games of life. Not writing Success Stories leaves this power solely in your own universe, often unavailable to be used in playing your games in life.

Reluctance to write Success Stories is a reluctance to utilize the win, ability or state in the physical universe. It is a reluctance to be successful in your games in life.

Making the writing of Success Stories painful is a major act of sabotage. Such things as: being hit for writing Success Stories, demanding false Success Stories, refusing to ask for Success Stories, making less or nothing of Success Stories, invalidating or ridiculing Success Stories, and more, are all acts of sabotage.

These acts sabotage you, and your power, by blocking your ability to bring into the physical universe and utilize your regained awareness, knowledge, abilities, and states in your games in life. They make you success reluctant.

Do not let the tacit or overt saboteurs win. Push through any reluctance you may already have and write Success Stories on every win, regained ability, or recovered state you have.

If this is still hard for you to do run:

Connected to Success Stories what have you done?

Connected to Success Stories what haven't you said?

If still resistive run:

Are there any unwritten Success Stories?

Tell me about it?

Write it up.

This will greatly enhance you to fully regain the use of your wins, abilities, states and power to win in the games of life.

ALAN C. WALTER

5 March 1997

UNPLEASANT SENSATION HANDLING

Unpleasant sensations, feelings, moods, even pain are factors in life. It is to be noted that unpleasant sensations, feelings, moods or pain can manifest at any time during study, and routinely do so for folks in their daily lives.

Unpleasant sensations, feelings, moods and pain knock you out of being present. Indeed, when you run the "Presence Process" for an extended period of time, it is quite routine for unpleasant sensations, feelings, moods or pain to begin to "turn on." Indeed, the Presence Process is used to benefit from this phenomenon. The reason being is that it is these unpleasant sensations, feelings, moods and pain that are an underlying cause of you not being as present, aware, competent and powerful as is your true nature.

Thus, one of the processes used in the restoration of your true full powers, presence, awareness and competence is the Presence Process (for extended time) with the Unpleasant Sensation Handling to deal with the unwanted unpleasant sensations, feelings, moods or pain that are in your way.

Some of our advanced processes for human development and ability enhancement directly ask for any unpleasant sensations, feelings, moods or pain that are connected to the area of ability or development being addressed.

When a person finds they have any unpleasant sensations, feelings, moods or pain in the way of their being fully present, being able to be fully aware with their attention under their control as they want, or preventing them from being able to direct their powers as they want; run this process:

First, have the person articulate or describe, as exactly as they can, the unpleasant sensation, feeling, mood or pain. Having them state or point to where it is located also helps.

Then run the following process by asking:

1)   What part of (named sensation/mood/pain) are you willing to experience?
Acknowledge the answer. Make no other comment.

2)   What part of (sensation/mood/pain) would you rather not experience?
Acknowledge the answer. Make no other comment.

Alternate these questions until the person has a win or is free from the sensation, or there is no more change happening (though the sensation/mood/pain should have diminished).

Then ask:

3)   What part of (sensation/mood/pain) are you willing to create? Acknowledge the answer. Make no other comment.

4)   What part of (sensation/mood/pain) would you rather not create? Acknowledge the answer. Make no other comment.

Alternate these questions until the person has a win or is free from the sensation, or there is no more change happening (though the sensation/mood/pain should have diminished).

This is quite a miraculous process. It restores to the person their ability to be present in the area and to be in control of the experience or creation of the unwanted sensation, mood or pain.   Generally, the unwanted sensation, mood or pain vanishes.

It is to be noted that, with the exception of physically caused pain due to illness or injury which benefit from medical treatment, most pain suffered by folks is spiritual in origin. It is because of this fact that the process above is so wonderfully workable. It is also true that physical pain is very often successfully handled with the above process, and such handling helps speed the physical healing.

CELEBRATION OF REGAINED ABILITIES, STATES AND WINS PROCEDURE

Definition:

CELEBRATE: *v.* 1. To observe (a day or event) with ceremonies of respect, festivity, or rejoicing. 2. To perform (a religious ceremony). 3. To announce publicly; proclaim. 4. To extol; praise.

American Heritage Dictionary

0.   Write up Success Story of all regained abilities, states and wins.

Take each ability, state or win and run:

1.   **Connected to (<u>regained ability, state, or win</u>), what powers have you recovered?**

      a.   **Have you ever used these powers to impress anyone?
How?
What were the consequences?**

      b.   **Have you ever used these powers to deny someone's impression on you?
How?
What were the consequences?**

      c.   **Connected to (<u>regained ability, state, or win</u>), what powers is it OK to use?**

      d.   **Connected to (<u>regained ability, state, or win</u>), what powers is it not OK to use?**

Repeat c. and d. to Cause Indicators.

2. a.   **Connected to (<u>regained ability, state, or win</u>), are there any unpleasant sensations?**

If so, get them named and do Unpleasant Sensation Handling on them.

      b.   **Connected to (<u>regained ability, state, or win</u>), are there any pleasant sensations you cannot easily experience?**

If so, get them named and do Unpleasant Sensation Handling on them.

      c.   **Connected to (<u>regained ability, state, or win</u>), are there any pleasant sensations that you must experience?**

If so, get them named and do Unpleasant Sensation Handling on them.

3.   Run Responsibility:

      a.   **Connected to (<u>regained ability, state, or win</u>), what are you willing to own and be responsible for?**

b.   **Connected to (<u>regained ability, state, or win</u>), what would you rather not own or be responsible for?**

Repeat a. and b. to Cause Indicators.

4.   a.   **Who would you be willing to know about this ability/state/win?**

b.   **Who would you rather not know about this ability/state/win?**

Repeat a. and b. until Cause Indicators.

c.   **What would be the consequences if it's known you have this ability/state/win?**

Repeat over and over to Cause Indicators.

5.   a.   **How valuable is this ability/state/win?**

b.   **If you can, put a monetary value to it.**

How much money would someone pay to get this ability/state/win? or

How much money will you make because of regaining this ability/state/win?

6.   **How can you implement these (<u>abilities/state/win</u>) now and in the future?**

Repeat 1 - 6 on each regained ability, state, and win until all are fully owned and willing to be used and known.

ALAN C. WALTER

27 August 1996
Revised 12 January 2001

Endnotes

1 *At a stroke, Pope Nicholas I denied your true spiritual presence, powers, virtues and potential as expressed in the original Trichotomy of Man, and relegated you to be a body and mind with a soul. The Trichotomy of Man that is now the doctrine of the Christian Church of the West is different to the original that is upheld by the Orthodox Christian Churches in the East. (It is worth noting the definition of orthodox here: 1) Adhering to the accepted or traditional and established faith, especially in religion. 2) Adhering to the Christian faith as expressed in the early Christian ecumenical creeds. Additional definitions are given in the American Heritage Dictionary from which this is taken.) This alteration of doctrine, along with altering the doctrine concerning the will of God, which before had been seen as passing through Christ from God, to state that God's will is the creation of Christ, is what caused the schism between the Roman West and orthodox East in the Church during the Papacy of Nicholas I. An enlightening book on these historical events is, The Spear of Destiny, by Trevor Ravenscroft.*

2 *Harvard Medical School's Dr. Jerome Groopman, author of "How Doctors Think," on PBS Channel 13 NewsHour with Jim Lehrer dated May 15, 2007. Dr. Groopman, in referring to why his book was written, stated: ". . . Misdiagnosis is remarkably common. 15% of all people are misdiagnosed. Some experts think it is as high as 20 to 25%. In half of all these cases there is serious harm to the person."*

INDEX

AVAILABLE TO OUR READERS

FREE VIDEO

Of

OUR WORKSHOP WITH LITERACY PARTNERS TUTORS

GO TO:

http://www.howtolearn-howtoteach.com/special-request/

Here you will actually be able to see how a group of teaching professionals responded to the live exercises and materials we presented in this book.

It was a lot of fun for all of them and us! Even if, a little surprising and a little embarrassing, for some at times, for these professionals to be experientially discovering what they have unwittingly been doing for so many years.

We even helped some debug their *OWN* earlier educational difficulties!

*****

BOOK ORDER

LECTURES, TRAINING & COACHING

Virginia and Roger are available for one–on-one counsel and guidance or help in the form of lectures or other training and address to groups including key note speeches.

For schools, home education groups, colleges, universities, non-profits, corporations or professional organizations, special editions of this book and discount rates for bulk orders are available.

Please contact us at:
www.abilityconsultants.com
rboswarva@abilityconsultants.com
vkoenig@abilityconsultants.com.

Mailing address:
162 West 13th Street
Suite 1
New York NY 10011
Telephone: 212 924 2619